THE FAITH OF OTHER MEN

Books by Wilfred Cantwell Smith

MODERN ISLAM IN INDIA
ISLAM IN MODERN HISTORY
THE MEANING AND END OF RELIGION

THE
FAITH
OF OTHER
MEN

WILFRED CANTWELL SMITH

HARPER TORCHBOOKS
Harper & Row, Publishers
New York, Evanston, San Francisco, London

Part I of this volume presents seven radio talks given, early in 1962, over the national network of the Canadian Broadcasting Corporation, in its series "The University of the Air." Part II is a lecture delivered in Montreal in 1961. They are presented here virtually as delivered, except that "this talk" has become "this essay," and "next week's talk" appears here as "our next chapter."

This book was originally published by New American Library in 1963. It is here reprinted by arrangement.

First TORCHBOOK edition published 1972.

STANDARD BOOK NUMBER: 06–131658–X

CONTENTS

I
The Faith of Other Men

II
The Christian in a Religiously Plural World

PART ONE

The Faith of Other Men

CHAPTER ONE

Introduction

For some years I used to teach in Lahore, a city that is nowadays the capital of West Pakistan but at that time was a provincial centre of undivided India. I was on the staff of a Christian college; this means that the institution was Christian in name and in direction, and aimed at being Christian in spirit. The majority of the teaching staff, however, were Hindus, Muslims, and Sikhs; and so were the great majority of our students. The Christians among us were attempting to illustrate and to practise our faith; our colleagues of other communities, often reverent men, were willing to work with us towards constructing and maintaining a community—a community religiously diverse.

Such a situation meant that for each member of the college, all his living was set in a context of this religious diversity; living and thinking, teaching and learning, even worshipping. Everyone, staff or student, carried out his daily tasks and his deepest reflections in an environment in which the majority of his fellows were members of other and divergent religious groups. This had implications not only for the man of firm conviction. It was interesting also for the lukewarm and the sceptical. Among the students, even the would-be atheist sopho-

9

more found himself in a more complex and tricky position than had his counterparts at, say, the University of Toronto, where I myself had been an undergraduate some years earlier. In India as in the West many of the young were rebellious and impelled to reject; yet amidst all the variety what was one to reject? In what sort of God was one to choose not to believe? Also, the political situation at that time, just before the splitting of British India into the new dominions of India and Pakistan, kept one from drifting into any glib notion that religion is not important, that the task of building up a progressive society can be carried forward without bothering about what men believe. On the Hindu-Muslim question, as an economic issue and linguistic as well as social and political and religious, Indian nationalism presently ran into flaming disaster. This, and the fact that we were after all a missionary college, were enough to remind all of us that faith is a serious and fundamental matter, to be neither taken for granted nor dismissed, but to be wrestled with in all profundity. The problems of religious divergence were vivid in our group, and pressed hard.

Now in this matter of religious diversity, our college was, of course, typical of the city in which it stood; and indeed of India at large. I would like to suggest also that the situation is in fact representative of today's world, for all of us. Although we are coming to recognize it only slowly, in fact modern life for all mankind is more truly pictured by that situation in Lahore than it is by the sort of oversimplified religious society with which most of us are familiar. We are tempted to think of circumstances such as those that I have described as somewhat odd or remote. Instead, we should realize that for this latter part of the twentieth century with its 'one world', it is rather *our* background here in Canada and the United States that is partial and unrepresentative. The religious life of mankind from now on, if it is to be lived at all, will be lived in a context of religious pluralism.

This is true for all of us: not only for 'mankind' in general on an abstract level, but for you and me as individual persons. No longer are people of other persuasions peripheral or distant, the idle curiosities of travellers' tales. The more alert we are, and the more involved in life, the more we are finding that they are our neighbours, our colleagues, our competitors, our fellows. Confucians and Hindus, Buddhists and Muslims, are with us not only in the United Nations, but down the street. Increasingly, not only is our civilization's destiny affected by their actions; but we drink coffee with them personally as well.

Even in Canada. Two years ago a student in one of the theological colleges in this country found himself under the persuasive influence of a visiting Hindu swami. Resident in Edmonton, Alberta, these days is a Muslim preacher from Cairo, recently come to the mosque in that city. A Parsi is director of the Montreal Symphony Orchestra. In Toronto, an attractive Buddhist church is visited by many inquirers. Not long ago there a simple advertisement in the university students' daily brought many undergraduates together for a serious discussion-group series on the Buddha's teachings, led by a Japanese-born Canadian Buddhist priest. In the nineteenth century the Christian missionary effort spread around the world. Today, in the United States, missionaries *from*

India, Japan, and the Muslim world are to be found preaching their creeds to an inquiring generation. This development has barely begun in Canada as yet, but it is to be expected soon. Canadian parents have become accustomed to their sons' and daughters' being attracted away from the ancestral faith towards unbelief (or perhaps Marxism), but it is a new thing for them to find their children turning their attention to alternative ancient faiths.

I personally do not expect many conversions from one tradition to another anywhere in the world in the coming hundred years. Yet we may all confidently expect increasing encounters among the varying traditions; and consequent ferment within each group. It will become increasingly apparent, and is already essentially true, that to be a Christian in the modern world, or a Jew or an agnostic, is to be so in a society in which other men, intelligent, devout, and righteous, are Buddhists, Muslims, Hindus.

The problems that this new situation poses are not only intellectual—though they are that, and we need many good minds to work on them. The matter is equally moral, and social; and involves us all. Surely the fundamental human problem of our time is to transform our new world society into a world community. The technological and economic aspects of this are already vigorously under weigh. The political aspects, which are trickier, are getting attention, even if it is only partially successful. Yet the intellectual, moral, and spiritual aspects are no less important. Men who have lost their faith, or whose faith is inadequate to mankind's new responsibilities, will not be able to build and hold the new world order without which we perish. Nor can that new world order be the work of men whose only vision is to impose *their* particular scheme upon everyone else. That is the Communists' mistake; let us hope that in a subtler and less roughshod fashion it will not unwittingly be ours. It is a particular temptation for some types of liberal humanist or secular rationalist. Such men tend to believe that religious faith is a private matter or even an unimportant matter which ought not to obtrude; and assume that everyone else must agree with them, and that world co-operation can be built on this idea. Yet it is an idea that in fact most of mankind rejects.

The problem is for us all to learn to live together with our seriously different traditions not only in peace but in some sort of mutual trust and mutual loyalty. We sometimes forget that this means arriving at a point where outsiders can trust us, as well as one where we can understand, respect, and honour them. It means also arriving at a point—most of us are nowhere near it as yet— where we can appreciate other men's values without losing our allegiance to our own. The world has little profit from that broadminded relativist who accepts the diversity of men's loyalties because he feels that no loyalties are ultimately valid, nothing is inherently worth while. Modern relativism is sophisticated cynicism—and is a devastating, not a constructive, force. Intellectually, besides, it is poverty-stricken: no one has understood the diverse faiths of mankind if his so-called explanation of them makes fundamental nonsense of each one. That we men worship God in radically different ways is a matter much too profound for glib or supercilious treatment. It poses not only an intriguing intellectual problem, but a serious political and social and moral one. Any attempt to grapple with it must do justice not only to the diversity but to the primary fact that we do worship God.

This new world situation, with its multicultural dimensions, involves our political leaders, our intellectuals, our trading economy, our Colombo Plan engineers, and, in the end, all of us in our daily contacts. Fundamentally, I think it is hardly going too far to say that finally one must become a new type of person to live aptly in the new world community that is struggling to be born.

This is true on the religious level as on others.

How then are we to do this? Who can help us see our way in this new adventure? The universities of the world are beginning to take up these problems at the specialist level; and there is a growing body of academic analysis and objective scholarship in this realm. This is what is called 'comparative religion', though the discipline is known also by other designations.

In comparative religion, then, or under some other name, departments at McGill, at the University of Tokyo, more recently at Karachi and Harvard, more traditionally at Leiden and Paris, are collecting the data in this field of religious history, analysing it, attempting to present it in intelligible fashion, and applying themselves to the intellectual task of seeing the total situation truly and providing the ideas with which it can be intelligently met. This can be very technical and very specialized indeed.

The student approaching this field of study is likely to be daunted at first by the formidable range of languages

involved, and the degree to which psychological, soci-
ological, historical, and other considerations intertwine.
Soon, however, he is caught up in the fascination and
profundity of the exploration. Personally, I believe that
the problem posed in this area is at least as important
for mankind as that of nuclear physics; as intellectually
challenging, as intricate, as exciting, as consequential.
The forces with which these studies deal are as weighty
and as explosive; the endeavour to understand them is as
critical; the challenges are as new and as profound. For
those of us for whom man is ultimately more significant
than his environment, for whom his mind and spirit are
more crucial than the things that he controls, the questions are more basic than any atomic ones.

Comparative religion as a topic of disciplined schol-
arly study may be considered on three levels: discovering the outward facts; learning the religious meaning;
and drawing generalizations. I think it important to
clarify these: partly because confusion in this realm has
been common, and also in order to make clear what we
shall be attempting to do in this little book (and what
we shall not).

The first two levels are both concerned with the as-
certaining of data: discovering the actualities of the religious life of the various communities of mankind; in the
past, and today. You might expect this to be relatively
easy, but it is not so simple as one might suppose. This is
why I have spoken of it as at two levels: one of external
facts, one of interpretation and meaning. We must learn
what precisely have been and are the doctrines, institutions, and practices, the symbols and patterns, of the
world's various communities. We must further endeavour

to know what these things have meant to the system's adherents. It is one thing to know, for instance, that in Christian worship there is a cross; it is another to know what the cross means to the Christian who is worshipping. Something similar holds for other groups, other symbols, other ages. The purpose, then, is to know accurately the religious forms of a people, and to understand with imaginative sympathy the significance of these forms in the religious life of those for whom they have been avenues of faith.

A good deal of progress has been made over the past century in the former of these realms, the factual, so that we know a very great deal about the religious life and history of all mankind. Some progress is today being made in the latter realm, of appreciating faith; not much yet, but some. There are still people who would claim that no one can really understand a religion who does not believe in it. On the whole, however, it is beginning to be true that we can grasp just a little, at least, of how the world looks to a man whose faith is different from our own. The task is difficult and precarious, but I am convinced that it can be done. In any case, I am sure that it is worth trying, and it is here that I plan to put our emphasis in this series.

For a good while now Western man has been curious about other people's customs and beliefs, and an interest in what is called 'the religions of the world' has of late been lively. A certain fixed pattern has grown up, in which the panorama of man's religious life across the world is described under a series of headings: Hinduism, Buddhism, Confucianism, and the like—a number of separate systems, each one called a religion. It has been supposed that the way to understand men's religious life is to learn at least something about each of these various systems. You will probably be surprised to hear that I intend to challenge this approach. It would take a sizeable book to set forth my argument that this is not the best way to understand what is going on. This much can be said here: that it is possible to know a good deal about what are called the various religious systems, and still not to understand the people whose life they involve.

Anyway, this traditional pattern is not the one that I intend to follow. My aspiration is not to get you to understand, for instance, Buddhism; but to help you to understand Buddhists. And this means, basically, trying to help you to see the world as a Buddhist sees it. Another way of expressing the same point is to say that I do not propose to talk about other men's customs and beliefs, but about other men's faith.

Now this is in some ways more difficult, though I think it is correspondingly more rewarding. Those of you who have been influenced by the traditional type of presentation may perhaps feel disappointed that I do not offer a brief description or even outline of the various systems. Apart from my own conviction that this is not the quickest way to the heart of the matter, there is the further point that this type of systematic presentation is already available in a number of books, including paperbacks, so that anyone whose interest is in the systems as systems can readily find what he wants in a variety of sources. Probably many of you have already read some of them.

If inner faith rather than outward system is to be our concern, then, how are we to deal with it? The method that I have adopted is this, and I am hopeful that you may find it rewarding: I will choose one characteristic item from the system of each major group, an item that may serve in some small way to represent the faith of that community; and will explore with you the meaning that that item may have for those for whom it serves as an expression of their faith. The item will be of varying sorts—an image, a phrase, a ceremony; in each case we will examine it as a symbol. In this way I hope that we shall get some inkling of how what seems to us at first unfamiliar and even odd may on inquiry suggest to us how other people look at the world.

The world at which they are looking is, of course, the same world that you and I observe, both tangible and transcendent, concrete and spiritual. And the people who do the looking, Chinese, Indians, of the Near East, are basically the same kinds of person as are you and I. But the ways that we in the West have looked at the universe, whether Christians, Jews, or secularists, are very special ways of our own; and our endeavour here will be to try to apprehend how other men perceive the stars and their neighbours, the making of a living, love, death, moral conflict, and all that makes human life human and life.

The most important single matter to remember in all this is that ultimately we have to do not with religions but with religious persons.

Our aim in these essays, then, will be, basically, to arrive at a more vivid awareness of the religious quality of the lives of these persons, who are nowadays our neighbours. Hence our title, *The Faith of Other Men*. We shall be highly selective, both with regard to the communities that we single out for attention, and with regard to their highly complex and elaborate systems. In each case we can choose only one facet of these for consideration. In selecting communities, we are perhaps justified if we confine our attention to the four major groups that, along with the Jews and Christians, comprise the great bulk of mankind today; namely, Hindus, Buddhists, Muslims, and Chinese. Together, these headings would cover at the present time perhaps between 80 and 90 per cent of the world's population religiously. In the matter of the inadequacy of any one symbol to portray the faith of a people, I can only plead that in these studies I have come to believe that it is preferable to explore one part in some depth than to survey a wider field more superficially. The surest way to misunderstand a great religious tradition is to miss its profundity. I trust that, in pursuit of seriousness, you will be willing to sacrifice extension of coverage—especially if we are quite explicit and self-conscious that that is what we are doing. Let me assure you now, with both candour and force, that we shall inevitably be leaving out a great deal. Any tradition that has moved hundreds of millions of persons through many centuries—won their loyalty and awe, inspired their poetry and courage, preyed upon their gullibility and excused their foibles, teased their intellects and warmed their hearts—such a tradition is not to be summarized in a few paragraphs.

My plan, then, is to deal with our subject at what I have called the second of its three levels: that of men's faith. We shall more or less neglect the first level, the sheer presentation of facts, the level of outward religious system. There remains the third level of comparative-religion studies, of which we have not yet spoken. This may be called comparative religion proper: that is, the endeavour from a comparative study of all the diverse phenomena and their interpretation to induce some general truths. In view of men's religious diversity, what can one say of man's religiousness itself? One cannot study men's religious traditions comparatively until one has something before one to compare. After the attempt to understand the individual faiths comes the attempt to understand the fact of faith itself, in the light of its history—to understand it as a well-nigh universal human phenomenon, immensely diversified in particular, remarkably persistent in general. Once one has surveyed this vastly wide and profuse field, what emerges? Can one make any over-all sense out of so bewildering a panorama of facts? In their profundity, problems of this kind are beyond the range of this series. Yet we shall come face to face with some of them in Chapters Six and Seven, when we shall be dealing with the implications for Jews and Christians of the faith of other men, and shall be trying to formulate our conclusions.

There remains one dimension of the whole matter in which all three levels are involved: namely, the historical. Religiously, as in other matters, history is important—indeed, massively important. Of man's religiousness in general, and of each religious tradition in particular, both our own and other people's, one may ask not only what it is but what it has been. The question is large, at every level—including that of universal significance. For it turns out, on inquiry, that things were different yesterday from what they are today. By implication one may then ask as to what they may become tomorrow.

What may become of other men's traditions, and one's own; of their faith, and of faith in general? This is a large issue, and one that transcends our capacity to handle in our limited space. I should only like to touch upon it here in a fashion typical of our approach throughout, by considering just one illustrative point.

In later chapters, our concern will be men of faith today. For each community, however, we must remember that there is a long and rich historical background; and before the present communities ever arose there were previous traditions, some of them mighty and consequential, that have since disappeared. The history of religion is bewilderingly rich; and we cannot go into it. Yet we do well at least to remind ourselves at the beginning how incredibly ancient among men is the tradition of religious faith. For this reminder, let me single out one facet of the religious life of prehistoric man; namely, the burial of the dead.

At the present time every human society on earth has some formal ritual to deal ceremonially with the death of individual members. Not all practise burial. Certain groups observe cremation, and there are one or two other alternatives. But as we go back in time we reach a point when the whole of mankind buried its dead. It is possible to trace elaborate ceremonial in a virtually unbroken line, in various parts of the earth—both among primitive groups and in the great early civilizations (conspicuously in ancient Egypt). When one goes further and further back to five, ten, twenty thousand B.C., the pattern that one sees becomes less ornate. This has to do partly with questions of the survival of evidence, partly it is because procedures themselves seem to have been less evolved; though massive and meticulous tombstones, as well as other later symbolisms, go back into neolithic times. The use of red ochre is palaeolithic; as is burying a body facing westward, and interring jewellery and weapons in a grave along with a body. These are various customs that survive widely until today. And many of the burial practices evidenced from extremely early times, and even before the appearance of *homo sapiens* with Neanderthal man, are fascinating in their intricate detail.

Some years ago I had the privilege of standing in the Rockefeller Museum in Jerusalem before a case in which the plaster was still wet, setting the skeleton of *Palaeo-anthropus palestiniensis* or 'Mount Carmel man', dating somewhere from a hundred to two hundred thousand B.C. It had been found under a floor in a distinct exca-vated cyst, quite clearly buried. This is the earliest in-stance we have of human activity of a kind that today we call religious. While there is no way of knowing what went on in the minds or hearts of this man's fellows who took the trouble to bury him carefully, this much we can say: that present religious practices of mankind can be traced back for at least a thousand centuries in a continuous tradition.

Some observers have been quick to infer from burial a belief among ancient men in immortality. I do not find this cogent. Immortality is a somewhat sophisticated doc-trine, a rather late endeavour to express in the form of ideas men's attitude to life, death, and the human spirit. In any case it is a doctrine, a belief, perhaps a metaphor. We are often a little too ready to infer that primitive man was a philosopher, intellectualizing his attitudes.

Even today we would be shocked if someone we knew treated the corpse of a friend without any ceremony, whatever might be his beliefs. I think we would be safer to take this early burial as indicating that at the very dawn of human existence men, in the presence of the death of their comrade, felt—or, saw; or, shall we say, experienced—something more profound than the animal world for a hundred million years earlier had ever experienced. And having seen it, man has never forgotten it, through all his long history since. Each of us, anew each generation, and throughout the world, repeats and continues this until today.

This much at least we may say: that prehistoric burial shows that man from the very earliest traces of his beginning has recognized that there is more to human life than meets the eye, that the total significance of man is not exhausted within the six feet of space or sixty years of time with which he plays his part on the stage of earth. The sober observation of the historian now agrees with the insight of the philosopher and the faith of the saint, that man is not man until he has recognized that the proper response to death is poetry, not prose.

CHAPTER TWO

Hindus

IN INTRODUCING this series of essays, I said that we would look in turn at each of the great religious communities of man and would try to see something of their religious quality, not by endeavouring to present in each case the whole system, even in its main outlines—with inescapable superficiality—but rather by singling out one item in the system, to see whether we could interpret that one element meaningfully, so as to catch the flavour of the orientation that it represents. Not Hinduism, therefore, but the Hindus, as seen through one of their symbols—this will be our concern here.

Now, you might imagine that the value of such a method would turn in part on my success in selecting a truly representative element, one that is typical of the community's attitude at large. Clearly there is something in this point, and in fact in subsequent chapters—on the Buddhists, and then Muslims, and so on—I shall be trying to meet this requirement, choosing in each case for our exploration a facet of the tradition that is in some sense central, typifying the whole. We may learn something, however, from the fact that in this very first presentation we come upon what is, indeed, one of the first lessons one must learn; namely, that the various religious traditions of the world differ not only in content but in form; not only in the answers they give, but in the questions they ask. One has begun to understand the religious life of India only when one has recognized that on principle nothing can be typically Hindu. The sprawling variety is deliberate and serious. There is no system to which something can be central. And Hindus have felt there should not be. A persistent affirmation in India has been that there are as many facets of the truth as there are persons to perceive it.

The Hindu is taken aback at any suggestion that religious life should optimally be of some one pattern; that there is even in heaven an ideal to which all men's minds or hearts or wills ought to conform. At the very least, intellectuals among them will be expected to choose one sort of path; more emotional or devotional types, another; and moralists and activists still another. No one avenue that *we* may choose, therefore, will be typical of the Hindu community at large. Each symbol represents, at most, one group among others.

By considering any aspect of the Hindu complex, therefore, we should be considering some Hindus and omitting many, many others. I do not propose to try to circumvent this in any way, or to deplore it, or even to apologize about it. This very point is part of the truth of the total community. One has understood India's religious life better, not less, if one accepts cheerfully its bewildering variety.

We should not be restlessly in search, then, of elusive generalizations, in a realm where truth lies rather in particularities. The outside observer must learn to rejoice with the Hindus in the variety, or at least to understand the rejoicing of those to whom unity lies in God, not in something that the Westerner calls Hinduism.

There is the further point that sophisticated Hindus have tended to hold that the great mass of customs and beliefs, gods and temples, and all, that make up the so-called Hindu religion (*dharma*) are but one stage on an ultimate human journey that leads beyond these things. We should be stopping short of serious Hindu affirmation, therefore, if we paused at the level of the vast Hindu religious complex. I am going to leave all that aside, then, and deal rather with one part of one of the ways (there are several) by which a Hindu escapes from 'Hinduism' and beyond it into salvation. A Hindu is free to choose. I follow him, not by describing to you what he chooses from, which is vast; but by interpreting to you one item that he may perhaps have chosen.

I am being, therefore, selective, though not arbitrary, when I choose as our emblem a phrase, one that has been important and can be illuminating. It is a statement, and pertains to the life of the intellectual man of faith. This lends itself to our discussion and analysis here; perhaps more readily (for the moment, anyway) than would the orientations of devout and fervent Bhakti worshippers, or the serenity of the detached activist, or the ritual of the humble villager, all of whom and many others we regretfully, but significantly, leave out of consideration.

The phrase that I have chosen consists of three Sanskrit words, generally regarded in India as the most important sentence that that country has ever pronounced; the succinct formulation of a profound and ultimate truth about man and the universe. The phrase is: *tat tvam asi*. *Tat* means 'that'; *tvam* means 'thou'; and *asi*

26

is the second person singular of the verb 'to be'. 'That thou art'; *tat tvam asi*. It means, thou are that reality, thou art God. The same truth is expressed in other ways; for instance, in the famous equation '*atman* equals *Brahman*'— or the soul of man is God, or the Ultimate Reality, with a very large capital U and capital R; the really real. The individual self is the world soul. The soul of man equals the ultimate of the universe. 'Thou', or to use our more colloquial term, 'you'—(each one of you reading this book)—are in some final, cosmic sense the total and transcendent truth that underlies all being, *Brahman* who precedes and transcends God Himself, the Infinite and Absolute Reality beyond all phenomena, beyond all apprehension and beyond all form.

I have chosen this phrase partly because it has been so important in India. Certainly it has been historically consequential, reverberatingly so. It has been profoundly meaningful to generation after generation of brilliant intellects, many of whom have written great commentaries on it, and to century after century of consecrated personalities. For such men the assertion *tat tvam asi* has been a saving truth. Not only convincing, but liberating. Not only true, but powerful. Earthly temptations fall away. The fetters of sin and desire and ignorance are gone, mortality dissolves, in the vision that these words express.

So we are told. But I have chosen it also just because to us in the West, with our radically different intellectual and theological background, it sounds so strange. What on earth does this phrase mean? What even do *we* mean when we say, as we may say all too glibly, that certain Hindus believe this? I personally have long felt that we must be on our guard against listing a series of propositions that we say other people believe, and imagining that thereby we know their religion. We do not know what we are saying, and we would better keep quiet, until we grasp, at least in part, what they mean when they say it, and what it means to them. Unless we know and can feel and see what the universe looks like to a man who genuinely holds this view, then we have not understood that man, and we do not know his faith. What does it feel like to hold *tat tvam asi?* If we can authentically answer that question, we shall have gone a long way towards understanding one facet, at least, of Hindu religious life.

Tat tvam asi, 'That thou art'. These three words are the expression, manifestly, of a profound religious experience, and have been for many the ground of a profound religious experience. The first point for us to seize is that, however strange the affirmation may sound to us at first, it is not silly. *Tat tvam asi* has been affirmed by men of outstanding intelligence, certainly; by men of greatness, courage, and dignity. Also, and this is at least equally important, by men of genuine sincerity. Beginners are often in danger of supposing that Hindus believe such-and-such because it is part of Hindu doctrine; instead of recognizing, rather, that it has become part of Hindu doctrine because Hindus believe it, because this is their actual assessment of the world, careful, sincere, and accurate. The same applies, of course, to Buddhists, Muslims, and for that matter to Christians and Jews—though this principle applies rather less cogently, perhaps, in a dogmatic tradition, where men are asked to believe on authority. *Tat tvam asi* was originally formulated because some perceptive and outstanding religious person wrestled with the problems of life and thought, and finally came up with this report of how he saw the universe. It has persisted now for twenty-some centuries and has been cherished, because other men, too, have tested it, and found it satisfying—something by which one could live, and die. To see man and the universe in these terms, they have testified, is deeply rewarding, and also is self-authenticating. It is not easy to grasp what these words mean, they say, but it is worth the struggle; is worth all struggle. For once you have seen it, they report, all else falls into place and you recognize that here indeed is the final serenity, the final and solemn vision, beyond which nothing more is needed or desired.

Of course there is no particular reason why you and I should agree with those who say *tat tvam asi*. All I am arguing at the moment is that we should take them seriously. Indeed for the moment I am not suggesting that we should concern ourselves with whether or not the proposition is valid. Our business—and this is exacting enough—is simply to see whether or not we can contrive to understand it.

Perhaps after this introduction you will be disappointed when I admit, and yet it is high time that I do admit, that I myself do not fully understand it. Let me hasten to add that this is not, I think, as preposterous as it may sound. In fact, there would be something wrong in the situation if I did fully understand it, or even if I thought that I did. For the Hindus, to whom this particular tradition is significant, have held emphatically that the meaning of this phrase, seemingly so simple, is in fact exceedingly difficult; that only after long and arduous discipline does one gradually come, and that exceptionally, to apprehend its truth. Finally to understand it, they affirm, is to be saved.

Now to be quite frank, I am not saved, in this Hindu sense: 'liberated' is a better translation of their term, freed from all the burdens and curtailments of finite existence. No, I have not fully understood what they mean. And yet. . . . I am bold enough to talk about it because I have, I think, begun to understand.

Now if I admit that I have not fully understood it, you may ask, then how do I know that there is something there to understand? The answer here is, first, that many Hindus of manifest intelligence and dignity find it profound and serious, including my friends. Second, I myself keep finding more in it, as I go on exploring it— or more precisely, as I go on exploring the universe and human history, with, in part, this concept in mind. Even an outsider can recognize that here indeed is one of those insights into transcendence, and into human destiny, that offer those who take it seriously increasing richness and subtlety and an increasing numinous awareness. I said a moment ago that there would be something wrong if I did fully understand it. For this truth is a mystery—not in the philistine sense that it mystifies and baffles, but on the contrary in the religious sense that it illuminates, but progressively and always expansively; that as one handles it, there opens up before one facet after facet of previously unsuspected wisdom, and at the same time new depths of previously unsuspected, and as yet unplumbed, uncertainty—a continuing sense that there is still more and more to be explored. I do not fully understand it: this is an understatement. Let me say, rather more frankly, that

I do not much understand it. Yet I rather suspect that even Hindus, though they see in it vastly more than I do, do not fully understand it, either. And that this is part of what they mean when they say that it is a cosmic truth. Any proposition that is fully understood by the human mind, and is in that sense subordinate to it, must be a finite truth, not a religious one. Of a religious truth, one asks only that it prove itself true in so far as one has explored it, and that it constantly beckon one on to explore it further.

There is another problem here, however, which we must face. I see something in this *tat tvam asi* affirmation, all right; an increasing something as I go along. Yet it is still little enough, goodness knows; and it is what *I* see in it—or if you prefer, is what I see in life by means of it. How can I be sure that I am on the right track, then? How can I know that what it means to me is, so far as it goes, in the direction of what it means to Hindus? The important thing to recognize here is that I cannot be sure. Hindus understand this symbol as a religious truth, and I think that I am beginning to understand it in the same way, but conceivably I am wrong. Conceivably I am misleading myself, and you—a rather devastating thought, and yet one that should be taken seriously. I think this possibility of misunderstanding is seldom given as much weight as it deserves, whenever anyone attempts to interpret a religious faith other than his own.

We can all understand this more forcefully if we reflect on the attempts of outsiders to understand our faith. How many Hindus or Muslims or Jews understand what we Christians mean when we say that in Christ we find God revealed, and that in him we find the power to live and to love? How many Jews feel that Christians, for all our study and contact, understand the Jewish faith? Interreligious understanding is a new field of endeavour, still at a tentative and explorative stage.

Anyway, having warned you of these hesitations, I am going to do my best. I am going to try to convey to you, in a few words, something of what I have come to understand of *tat tvam asi*. If I succeed in enabling you to understand, in part, what I see here, and if I have succeeded in understanding, in part, what Hindus see, then our endeavour will have been worth while.

I propose, first of all, to take four areas of human life, and to tell how I see this equation applying in each; namely, the intellectual, the aesthetic, the moral, and the area of historical development and creativity.

First, in the sphere of intellectual truth. Every teacher, every parent, knows that there are two aspects of, say, a child's acquiring new truth; let us call them sincerity and validity. Sincerity is obviously quite fundamental; without it there is no education. To learn by rote is not really to learn at all. There is no point in a child's repeating parrot-like a proposition that he has been taught, if he does so coldly and mechanically, without understanding it, without having appropriated it to himself. It is really a form of cheating if a child scores marks on an examination by reproducing an answer that may externally be correct, but that he himself does not believe or does not understand. We call a man a liar if, and only if, he says what he himself believes to be false. Certainly in any personal sense, there cannot be intellectual truth unless the person who intellectualizes appropriates the truth to himself and assimilates it, interiorizes it in full sincerity. Surely each one of us must strive for full intellectual integrity in our intellectual life.

At the same time, however, we must strive, equally and utterly, for full objective validity. If a proposition is of no value to us unless we make it our own, also it is of no value to us unless it is externally true; unless it matches the actual facts of the outside world. We may escape being liars by being gullible to our own deceptions, but we shall not escape being fools. The utmost rigour of external accuracy, the utmost rigour of internal sincerity, combine to lead us to truth. I do not know whether you agree with me that only this combination can get one anywhere in science. I hope that you will agree that in all personal life, including religious, the combination is where truth lies.

Certainly our goal is, must be, that we should say, whether to our neighbours or to ourselves, only what we genuinely and deeply believe, and that we should believe only what is actually true. Subjective honesty, objective validity. In so far as you achieve that, intellectually you are saved. *Tat tvam asi.*

Again, let us take the life of art. Here, what a foul bog of insincerity must be swept away before there can be any hope of beauty in our lives. What a lot of people, it has been remarked, will say that Milton's *Paradise Lost* is a great poem who have never read it or if they have read it have been bored stiff. Modern life is subject to enormous pressures to aesthetic insincerity, from the disk jockey to the classroom, from the art gallery to the billboard, all pushing men to accepting as valuable not what they value but what others praise; pushing us away, that is, from all true aesthetic awareness. I am lost to beauty except in what is beautiful to me—genuinely, sincerely. Surely we must train our children not to *believe* that X is beautiful, but to see that it is, to appreciate it, deeply and inwardly and truly and personally.

In modern times, this side of the argument is more readily accepted than the other, which has gone out of fashion rather, but in my view is equally fundamental; namely, that I aspire not only to see things as beautiful myself, but also to see as beautiful what is beautiful, really, and only that. There is no point in my children growing up believing that Mozart is better than the raucous rampage of rock 'n' roll, if they are merely repeating this on my authority, or in order to gain prestige, and do not feel it in their bones when they hear the two. They must learn to be sincere, utterly and relentlessly, in their musical as in their other judgements. Yet neither is there any point in their growing up to be sincere, if they come to prefer in fact the jig-jag assault of most commercial radio to Mozart. For then they would be wrong. I want them to know that Mozart is better, if indeed I am right in believing that he is, because they themselves have come to see that he is better, because they can themselves hear the greater beauty that is in fact, objectively, there. My goal is to recognize as lovely what is in fact lovely, without deceiving myself and without being deceived—once again to combine integrity and validity, subjective judgement with objective truth.

As I say, nowadays this position is less widely held, since many people have lost their faith that beauty is sensed. This does not invalidate my argument, but in objectively given, in addition to being subjectively fact clarifies it, if you recognize that this is, indeed, a loss of faith. Those who deny the objective or absolute reference in aesthetics are rejecting the transcendent or divine quality of beauty, are failing to see it as something more than mundane. Those, on the other hand, who worship a god of beauty will quickly see the point; as will those who, being monotheist, see the God of beauty as being finally identical with the God of justice or truth or love, so that in our awareness of beauty, we are reaching out to touch the hem of His garment. Those of you who do *not* see beauty as absolute, and do *not* hold that man's aesthetic judgements are right or wrong in ultimately the same sense as our judgements of fact, will perhaps be the first to recognize that the absolutist position I am putting forward is, indeed, a religious affirmation. This is really all that I am asking you to see.

I personally am persuaded that some things are in fact more beautiful than others, and that my task is to discover which is which, in genuine appreciation. My task, and my salvation. For those who share this conviction, this faith, one's soul is saved, musically speaking, when one can within oneself actually see and hear, in deep personal response, the excellence of such music as is objectively excellent. Your goal is to attain an inner appreciation of an outer reality; a personal sense of an impersonal truth; to appropriate as your own a cosmic quality. Ideally, *tat tvam asi*. Ultimately, you and It must coincide.

Turning next to morality, we need not belabour the discussion since the point is similar and clear. It can be debated, for instance, whether in training our children in the moral life one should begin by stressing that some things are imperative, others wrong, so that they must learn to do, and to do only, what is inherently right, and then gradually, as they get older and more responsible, lead them to develop their own moral sense and subjective discrimination and conscience; or whether, contrariwise, one should begin by stressing sincerity and honesty and personal choice, leading them gradually to a developed discernment, an increased maturity, so that their genuine choices will be more and more reliable. Probably most of us aim at combining the two, in a happy synthesis. In any case, wherever one may begin, surely there is no debate about where ideally one ends: namely, at a total integration of sincerity with the moral law.

I am not moral if my act merely conforms to external standards that I myself have not accepted, if I act without inner conviction. Yet neither am I moral if I am merely paving the road to Hell with my well-meaning stupidities or even wickednesses. Here again, of course, some people have lost their faith that transcendent moral standards do exist. Others have lost their faith that total honesty is utterly essential. It is good religious insight, however, to discern that both are imperative. You must do what *you see* to be good; and you must see to be good what actually is good. To contravene either is to sin. To have both is morality. *Tat tvam asi.*

Similarly, finally, in creation. The artist, the statesman, the theologian, the bricklayer, must construct in conformity with inner standards and with outer. Canadian foreign policy is perverse, except in so far as it can combine being authentically Canadian with being truly apt to the outside situation. The whole of evolution is sound or awry, in so far as its inner *élan vital* is or is not both genuine and authentic, both spontaneous and appropriate.

So much, then, for this argement. This presents part of what I see in this famous phrase.

Turning to a more theological concern, there are elements in Christian and Jewish doctrine that from quite another angle may help us to see the point of the Hindu formulation. Take, for example, the Biblical principle of *imago Dei*, the image of God: that man has been created in the likeness of God—a doctrine that is crucial, profound, and of inexhaustible moment. Or take our Christian doctrine of incarnation, which involves the discernment that God is truly known in the form of man, who represents 'true' humanity. Admittedly in the Christian tradition there is also the doctrine of sin, carried in Calvin's case to that of total depravity; but even this can perhaps be seen as another way of saying what the Hindu is saying in *tat tvam asi*. For the Hindus certainly assert that this truth is a hidden, final truth, not an overt, immediate one. Man's true self, they hold, is divinity. But man's empirical self, his actual mundane personality, is part of *maya*, the distracting, illusionary realm of phenomena, that obscures from mortal eyes the transcendent truth beyond. You must overcome your empirical self and realize a cosmic universal beyond it. 'Not I, but Christ that liveth in me', as Saint Paul put it.

Again I may be wrong but I see a parallel between the Christian doctrine of man's sin and depravity and this Hindu doctrine of man's essential divinity as contrasted with his existential humanity. I also allow myself, however, to speculate about another possible parallel, at first blush equally paradoxical. We Christians affirm that God is personal, and we give great weight to this major affirmation. Hindus affirm that *Brahman* is impersonal. It would take us too far afield to explore what they mean when they say that (or what we mean when we say the other). I think that both mean something rather special. Anyway, our affirmation that God is personal bears, I believe, some relation to, and may help us to see at least part of the point of, their concomitant faith *tat tvam asi*.

There are facets in all this that could be discussed at enormous length. Please do not let me close having given an impression that I have tried to satisfy you on this issue. I shall have succeeded in my effort if I have helped us to see the sentence *tat tvam asi* as a religious symbol, meaningful to man and one that can repay serious attention.

CHAPTER THREE

Buddhists

In this series I am selecting from each religious community, in order to interpret its faith, a single symbol, in the hopes that through it we may gain an insight into the religious life of those for whom it is meaningful.

For the Buddhists, I have chosen a ceremony, and I will try to present it as it is enacted in a Burmese village. We will then see if we can uncover part at least of what it means to those involved.

Burma is a Buddhist country, and every village has its monastery—or temple or shrine: it is a little difficult to know what to call it, since any of our terms can be a trifle misleading. Anyway it is a Buddhist centre, 'set in a bamboo grove, flanked by shady mango trees', in a characteristic architectual form, with a seven-roofed apex. It is usually just outside the village proper, not too close, not too far away: far enough to symbolize its quality of sanctity, representing an order of life different from the day-to-day routine of the people, set just apart from it, and yet near enough to be relevant, concerned with the people's problems. Coming and going between the village and the monastery are easy and natural, but are not unconscious. Between the norm of what ought to be and the actuality of everyday life, between the abiding and the transient, the sacred and the profane, the relation is close, yet the two are not identical. Not two different worlds, but two aspects of the life of man. The monastery is the village school (and literacy in Burma for both men and women has for almost a thousand years been remarkably high); it is the village dispensary, social centre, retreat, old people's home, counselling service, as well as moral and spiritual focus. In the building or just nearby will be found a statue of the Buddha, the unruffled calm of which portrays and promotes the serenity of the monks' slightly withdrawn but dedicated life of service.

The ceremony that I wish to present is what may be called an initiation or confirmation rite for boys, at puberty or earlier. There is a corresponding rite for girls, but we shall consider only the one. It (the boys') is called *Shin Byu*. In broad sweep it compares to 'joining the Church' or First Communion or Confirmation in the Christian pattern, *Bar Mizvah* in the Jewish, and to related ceremonies throughout the world. But let us see the particularity of the Burmese Buddhist practice.

In essentials it is a re-enactment of the Going Out ceremony of the life of Gautama the Buddha. Most of you know that story: how Siddhartha Gautama, who was later to become the Enlightened One, the Buddha, was born the son of a king and grew up in a palace surrounded by opulent luxury, living in secure ease with the warm affection of his parents and the admiring service of all his associates. His father, the raja, having heard it foretold that this child might forsake the world to become a hermit, and finally a great religious teacher and saint, sought to forestall this by protecting him from

all knowledge of misery and all contact with pain, and
gave strict orders that his son should know only the de-
lights of life. Gautama grew up and matured, and in due
course he was married to a lovely princess, and presently
they were blessed with a charming baby son. All was
going exceedingly well; here was a young man well
favoured and well established, seemingly with everything
that man's heart could desire. But then, of a sudden, the
prince, as he was being driven in his chariot through the
park, by misadventure met a broken old man, then a
beggar, next a sick man, and finally a corpse; and his
charioteer, on being questioned, explained to him these
phenomena of decrepit old age, destitution, sickness, and
death, and further explained that yes, all men are subject
to these ills. Gautama was profoundly troubled in spirit,
and went home pondering. The ills of mankind, of which
he had now become aware, preyed on his mind; till
eventually one night—and this part of the tale is told
with vivid artistry, in story and in picture, throughout
the Buddhist world—one night he got up, took one last
loving look at his sleeping wife and beloved child, and
went out—out into the world in search of an answer to
man's sorrow. This Going Out, or The Great Renuncia-
tion as it is also called, is the prototype for our Burmese
village ceremony, which commemorates this act by
which Siddhartha Gautama went out from palace and
home, wife and family, wealth and contentment, and
turning his back on these mundane satisfactions, set
forth on his spiritual quest, to seek out a remedy for
men's ills. The rest of the story, presupposed, is of
course also relevant; that he not only sought but found
—found the answer to all men's questioning and all

men's need; to become, in Buddhist eyes, the Saviour of the world.

In the *Shin Byu* ceremony today in Burma, then, this well-known and well-loved scene is re-enacted, with the young village boy playing the role of the hero. It is a gala day, the whole village colourful and boisterous in festival mood and gay attire. The child is fitted out in princely garb, his family and friends feast his coming of age, rejoicing, and then at a certain point in the ceremony the child bids farewell to his family, takes off his gorgeous clothes, to replace them with the saffron robe of the monks' order, and is led away from the village to the monastery, where he is received as an inmate. He then lives in the monastery, for a length of time that is altogether unfixed. Some boys stay for only a token period of a few weeks, others remain for some years, as, in effect, boarders in a residential school as well as novices in a monastery, while a few may remain for the rest of their lives, having taken up the monastic career as their own.

This, then, is the ceremony.

We have called it 'a symbol', since it is a religious ceremony. Within the pattern there is a meaning, a deep and intangible significance that is symbolized; beyond the forms there is substance, or the intimation of a transcending, limitless truth, an infinite that becomes available to men within the finite, through these channels that a society inherits and cherishes, and uses to express its faith and to nourish it. Can we learn something of that faith, and appreciate in part that inner meaning, by exploring the significance of these outward forms? This is the task of comparative religion: not only to ascertain the institutions, beliefs, and practices of a tradition but to ascertain also, if one can, what these things mean to those who participate in them. Religious truth lies not in symbols but in what is symbolized—if only we can apprehend it.

Two preliminary observations are in order. The first is that of course we cannot apprehend it fully. Not only can the outsider never grasp in its entirety what a tradition means to those within it, but even those within, as we suggested in our last chapter, never apprehend *fully*. This is altogether proper; since, after all, religious symbols symbolize the infinite, or at the very least symbolize what is greater than man. The whole point of any religious tradition lies in the fact that it introduces man to what is greater than he and greater than itself.

Our second observation is that this ceremony, and indeed any Buddhist symbol, and indeed every religious symbol in whatever tradition, can mean different things, at different levels, to various men—and here, to various boys. There is more behind our own tradition, and behind other peoples', than any one man can grasp. Meaning is determined in part for each participant by his particular experience, and by his capacity, sensitivity, imagination, intensity, and whimsy. We can generalize, but we should remember that that is what we are doing. The *Shin Byu* ceremony in Burma would be different from every other religious ceremony in our own or any other tradition if it could not mean somewhat different things to different men. All interpretation, then, must be suggestive rather than conclusive.

Having said these two cautionary things, however, we can go on in an attempt to interpret. And indeed in part this is fairly easy to do. For any of us, particularly if we have religious faith ourselves, even if it be of another variety, can fairly readily appreciate something, at least, of what is here involved. With only a minimum of imagination we can transpose elements so as to grasp the human significance.

From the point of view of the parents, for instance: as with any comparable rite, here the parents are participating in that profoundly moving experience of dramatically expressing their handing over their son from their own personal charge to that of the society, and in a sense handing him over to his own, to be in charge now of himself. They are enacting the transition by which he *becomes* (that word is so disarmingly simple!), becomes no longer the child of a Buddhist, which is one thing, profoundly meaningful, but a Buddhist, which is another, equally profoundly meaningful. Yet the ceremony symbolizes also that their son is not only leaving their care to enter a new phase, of his own responsibility, but is doing so under the same auspices as have been their own. The child identifies himself with the Buddha, the Eternally Wise One, as they themselves have long since done; and subordinates himself to the traditional norms of their society, crystallized in the monastery, as they themselves have long since done. It would be a very different wrench for those parents if their child were seen as, even symbolically, leaving their care to set out on an independent career entirely on his own, an unrelated centre of unguided new directions. Instead, they see him as humanly independent, yet oriented in what they regard as the cosmically right direction, free of their control but accepting as they have done in free commitment the guidance of a transcending wisdom.

A religious tradition formulates, of course, into a pattern whatever those within it have valued, have found worth pursuing, worth knowing, worth admiring. And it is a thrilling and solemn moment to see one's son cut the ties that relate him directly to his parents and at the same time turn his face in the direction that those parents have found supremely to be good. There may well be, or even must be, an inner hope that the child will discover and realize values within or through the cherished order that one has oneself missed, either to perceive or to attain. But one's knowledge that such values are there, of wisdom, comfort, joy, and truth, in inexhaustible measure, means that one rejoices to see the child set out in quest of them.

As for the boy himself, I will not try to speculate as to what goes on in his mind, at either the conscious or unconscious level. How much he personally has been moved, in his home or at previous village ceremonies, by the stories of the Buddha; how sensitive he has been, in such contacts with the monastery or the monks as he has had, to the numinous quality of life, crystallized in these sanctities—such things will vary, of course, from boy to boy. How deep an impression the day will make on him; how seriously he takes the moment when he doffs the splendid gala attire, to take on instead the austere garb of the monastery; how touched he may be with some spiritual overtones or simply with nostalgia or mischief, as he says good-bye to his parents and sets his face towards the monastery—I leave you to judge. His later

development, year by year, as it unfolds or as he unfolds it, will determine of course in part whether he
gradually lets slide or minimizes or even forgets these
matters, or alternatively, perhaps, spends his life slowly
exploring them, to discover step by step the increasing
richness and depth of the spiritual life and little by little
the profounder meanings behind the symbols.

If he becomes, for instance, in modern times, a medical
doctor, having gone off to the big city for his education
and even perhaps abroad; or if he becomes a modern-
type professional social worker, or whatever it may be—
then who can tell how far the motivation for his career,
and the constancy and integrity and devotion with which
he pursues it, may be influenced by his experience at
this ceremony—or by having grown up in a village and
in a home where such a ceremony is traditional?

Yet we ourselves, I would suggest, even without being
Buddhist, can discern and consider together briefly two
at least of the major connotations of this ritual.

One of these raises the question of what one means
by speaking of the truth or otherwise of a particular
religious orientation. The *Shin Byu* ceremony itself, as
acted out in a modern Burmese village, is of course a
ceremony, a rite. It is not in itself true or false. But it
represents something; and one can perhaps ask whether
the something that it represents is true or false. One can
also ask how truly it represents it. And this, I suppose,
turns on the quality of those taking part, how seriously
and competently and devoutly they do so, and the like.
And with what sincerity. I have long thought that one
should not speak of a religion's being true or false
simply, but rather of its becoming true or false as each

participant appropriates it to himself and lives it out. It is much too glib to say that Christianity, for instance, is true (or, indeed, is false) without recognizing that my Christianity may be more false than my neighbour's, or that so-and-so's Christianity may be truer today than it was last year. I believe that this point is of much greater seriousness than we usually recognize: and for our present purposes, we should note in passing that the Buddhism of one Burma village is truer in a particular celebration of the *Shin Byu* ceremony of one year than it is in another, or than in another village.

Yet beyond this there is a second question, which some people would call a prior question (though I am not sure about that), as to whether that which is being represented is, in principle, true.

What about the Going Out episode itself, then, as an event in the life of Siddhartha Gautama? If we ask whether this is true, there are again several levels. At the level of prose and of history, modern scholarship is as usual sceptical but uncertain. Probably there was an actual historical figure of this name, about the sixth century B.C., quite possibly he was a prince, in at least a petty kingdom, and it is not at all unlikely that, as was a custom in India at that time, he left home in search of spiritual wisdom. The details of his life are so mingled with legend in the accounts that have come down to us that the sceptic cannot separate the two, and is left with a commanding personality, about whom we know for certain the immense impact of his faith and teaching on his followers, but not at all for certain any specific details of his career. This is one reason why I said just now that I am not sure that there is here a *prior* question. The details of this actual ceremony are perhaps on the same sort of plane, so far as prosaic historical truth is concerned, as are those of our Christian celebration of Christmas. In both cases I personally would be concerned rather with the poetic than with the prosaic truth. The shepherds and the star can be made spiritually true today (or sometimes, spiritually false), quite regardless of their historical truth in 4 B.C. So, I think, with the Buddha.

I would suggest, then, that in the Going Out myth there is, in fact, truth; a psychological truth of almost universal validity—and that one need not be a Buddhist to see this. The transition of the Buddha from the protected innocence of the home, with its ease and security and comfort, to the painful realities of adult life, is psychologically true for all men, is it not? and not merely for those born in palaces. At some point in the life of all of us there comes an awareness of old age and poverty and sickness and death. To some it comes earlier than to others, to some more dramatically and all at once than to others. But we all discover at some time in a serious, personal, realistic fashion that we and our friends are liable, indeed are destined, to these ills. And do not all of us parents try to shield our children at the first, at least, from this sorrow? At the *very* first, of course, they are shielded by their own immaturity, the child's inherent incapacity to grasp what is happening, even if decrepitude and illness and death occur right beside him. Later, we as parents give them what comfort and what happiness we can—little enough, perhaps, but we do protect them, with greater or less success, against the onslaughts of an otherwise tough world. We ourselves were protected for a time in our parents' home; but since, we have *come out* of that security and ease into the realities of maturity.

There is, then, I suggest, in universal human terms, a psychological truth in the Buddhist Going Out ceremony—a truth that Burmese villagers do well to re-enact and to re-ponder.

My second point, however, would go further: that there is in universal human terms a moral and spiritual truth here, too. The renunication of wordly values, in favour of wisdom and spiritual perception—this also, surely, is common in some form to all moral and religious life. Each one of us can set out in quest of moral values and spiritual goals, only if we renounce the immediate mundane rewards of spiritually unenlightened existence, in some fashion, at some point, with more or less sudden and more or less conscious volition and decisiveness. And the sooner, the more dramatically, the more forcefully a growing boy learns this lesson, surely the better. Again this particular representation overdramatizes, perhaps, oversharpens the contrast. I personally have been struck and even troubled, I will confess, that the price paid by Gautama included leaving his family, as though wife and child were a drawback instead of a help in spiritual and moral life. Yet those of us who are fortunate in this regard must not complacently forget that Christ also made the same point, in a comparably radical, over-strident way: '. . . Unless a man leaves his own father and mother and wife and children and brothers and sisters . . . he cannot be my disciple . . .' . To opt for truth and goodness is a decision that must involve a willingness, at least, to surrender everything else—everything.

Finally, there is the still further point that the *Shin Byu* ceremony is the act not only of an individual, and of a social community, but also of a religious order. The role, in this ritual, of the child—Everyman's son—symbolizes that each one of us is involved, at first hand, in this drama of living on earth, participant on the one hand in its tumults and its vicissitudes and exactions and its routines, its transience and decay, but participant also in an enduring quality that transcends the mundane, and lifts us, or can lift us, out of the utterly contingent; and that this quality is moral. And that in righteous living man has a window on eternity.

This point applies to everyone individually, and must be re-enacted over and over again as each new generation, each new person, comes along. It applies to every society, so that the whole community participates in each one of its members' personal involvement; and does so again and again.

Nonetheless, it is not only the person, and not only the group, whose involvement constitutes the ceremony. They are accepting it, and repeating it; but they are not creating it. They are involved, but it is oriented not to them, but to the Buddha. In the identification with him they are affirming that their recognition of the moral law is not their own whim, and is not just their society's tradition; rather it is given to them, by someone who, they affirm, not only like them set out in this direction, but, unlike them, arrived at the goal. There is a subtlety here, and I am not confident that I can make my meaning clear. The faith of Buddhists is involved and there is virtually nothing in our Western tradition to help us to see the validity or even the significance of a religious faith that we do not share. Yet let me try: I personally see a profound significance in the fact that these Buddhists are identifying themselves with a man who, if only in their own assertion, not only went out in search of Truth, but found it, so that their assurance of the validity of 'going out' rests not merely on their sense of adumbrations of eternity, but on an equal and final assurance that the going does in fact lead somewhere.

People without faith, or without firm faith, sometimes speak of religious traditions in terms of man's search. This is not adequate for traditions such as the Christian or Jewish or Islamic, which rest on a concept of revelation; but neither is it quite adequate here, for although these Buddhists do not talk of revelation and do not even talk of God, yet they keep their tradition alive by bringing to it afresh each generation, for now twenty-five hundred years, a live conviction that their quest is not merely a quest, but is guaranteed as it were by the Buddha's Buddhahood.

I wonder whether you see the importance that I do in the living assurance here that someone has shown the way, having travelled it. Therefore this is not a guess, but a discovery; not a groping, but a joyous affirmation. Now, this remains true, and you and I can recognize it as such, quite apart from any question of whether or not we are Buddhists. Our capacity to see its significance and even its validity does not turn on our accepting any doctrine about the Buddha. One might almost be tempted to say that this aspect of the ceremony is made true not by what the Buddha accomplished, but by the faith of men in his having accomplished it. Certainly their faith, today, in what transcends themselves is crucial, and is creative. We need not agree with them on any metaphysical role that the Buddha played in the past, in actual history; and yet we may recognize the metaphysical role that he is playing today in the lives of these men. And we may recognize the significance of their faith—and in this faith even an outsider may share—that such a role is ideally there, to be filled. What I am suggesting is that there is a metaphysical truth in these Buddhists' faith, which is independent of the historical truths of their belief.

I close, then, hoping that perhaps this brief presentation may have helped you to feel that once you have learned the form, you yourself could reasonably participate, at least imaginatively, in such a ceremony as the *Shin Byu*, or at least could sympathize with those who do; that here, something within each of us is significantly touched, so that this ritual of a distant group makes sense.

And may I add that the more genuine and more live our own personal religious faith—in my case Christian—the more sense it makes?

CHAPTER FOUR

Muslims

ALMOST ANY VISITOR to India interested in the religious
life of its people will note a striking difference ar-
chitecturally between a Hindu temple and a Muslim
mosque. The temple is apt to be ornate, even florid. Its
involute complexity suggests that truth is much more
elaborate than one had supposed, and denies nothing, not
even incongruity. Very different is the stark simplicity
of the Muslim place of worship. The mighty Imperial
Mosque in Delhi, for example, is a structure whose ar-
tistic impressiveness and power come from the use of
straight lines and simple curves, splendidly graceful and
yet austerely disciplined. Certainly it is brilliantly conceived and its impact is immediate: one grasps at once
the balance and dignity, the spacious reverence, the
serenity of its straightforward affirmation. Its architect's
vision of the glory of God, and of man's service due to
Him, is evidently an ordered vision.

Such a point is confirmed if one has the privilege of
witnessing a service in such a mosque, especially at one
of the great festival prayers, where perhaps a hundred
thousand people array themselves in neat lines and bow
in precise unison as token of their personal and corporate
submission to the will of God, which is definite and sure.

A similar contrast can be seen in the realm of doctrine. For a Hindu, there are various systems of ideas, involute, elaborate, and always tentative, from among which he may choose. In contrast, the Muslim community symbolizes its belief in probably the simplest, tidiest creed in all the world. I am sure that you have all heard it: 'There is no god but God, and Muhammad is God's apostle'. The Muslims themselves refer to this simply as 'the two words', or even 'the word'. And while this may be carrying compression just a trifle far, still its two pithy clauses are, certainly, as succinct and clean as one could hope to find.

Because of its centrality, and its neatness, this simple creed may well provide us with the item for our consideration of the Muslims. As with other religious communities, so with the Islamic, we choose one element from out the formal pattern of their faith, in the hope that, exploring it, we may find that it can lead us, if not to the heart of their religious life, at least into its precincts, and can suggest something of the richness of what lies behind. What better emblem of the Muslim's faith, for our purposes, than this crystallized creed, which the Muslims themselves have chosen to sum up their belief? To repeat this creed is, formally, to become a Muslim; perhaps to understand it is to understand a Muslim. Or let me put the point more realistically: to begin to understand it may be to go some distance, at least, towards understanding the position of those whose faith it typifies.

In suggesting the coherence and simplicity of the Muslim confession of faith, I do not wish to suggest that it is limited or lacks profundity. A mosque may be very intricately decorated—fine interlacing arabesques and the endlessly delicate complexities of an elaborate calligraphy usually embroider the arches and the walls —yet these decorations, however ornate in themselves, are regularly held in strict subordination to an over-all pattern that is essentially simple, so that detail is organized into a coherent unity. Similarly in the realm of doctrine. The Muslim world has produced its philosophers and theologians, constructing elaborate systems of ideas—the names of Avicenna and Averroes are probably the best known in the West, but there are many others also who worked out in careful detail considerable structures of thought. And there were also meticulously elaborate systems of law, comprehensive and ramified. But again, these were subordinate to the higher truth, the simpler truth, of the creed.

As one gets closer to truth, one gets closer to God; and God is one. He is majestic, mighty, awesome, merciful, and many other things, but above all, for the Muslim, He is one. Every other sin, the theologians affirm, may be forgiven man, but not that of *shirk*, polytheism, the failure to recognize that the final truth and power of the universe is one.

Before we turn to questions of meaning, which are of course our chief concern, let us note a few points about the formula as a formula. I suppose that every effective religious symbol is not only inexhaustibly meaningful in what it stands for, but is also in some ways intrinsically interesting in itself. This one certainly is. We have already remarked that it is short. It is also pungent and crisp. In the original Arabic—the language in which it is always used, no matter what the actual language of the people concerned, from Indonesian to African Swahili, from South Indian Malayalam to Turkish—in Arabic it is resonant and rolling, packing quite a punch. It so happens that of the fifteen syllables, about half begin with an *l* sound, or end with it, or both. This liquid alliteration, added to the rhyme, and to a very marked rhythm, is quite forceful. *Lā-'i-lā-ha-'il-lal-lāh; Mu-ḥam-ma-dur-ra-sū-lul-lāh.*

Then there is a calligraphic point. In the Arabic alphabet, which is anyway highly decorative, it so happens that this particular set of words when written out is strikingly patterned, and lends itself to very picturesque presentation.

The formula is certainly in constant service. For example, it is whispered in the ears of the newborn baby, so that its affirmation may be the first words that a Muslim shall hear on entering this world. And between then and its use at his funeral, he will hear it, and pronounce it, often and often and often. And apart from its ceremonial and—as it were—sacred use, it can be found in everyday affairs also. I remember a scene in India some years ago when my wife and I were one summer at a mountain resort in the Himalayas, and were out for a hike in the hills; we came upon a work-gang busy in the construction of a rude mountain road. It was, of course, all hand labour; they had crushed the stones with hammers, and were now rolling them with a large and very heavy roller. Rather in the fashion of sailors working to a sea shanty, they were rhythmically pulling this heavy roller in spurts of concerted effort: the foreman would sing out *Lā ilāha illa 'llāh*, and the rest of the gang, then, would put their shoulders to the ropes and with a heave would respond *Muhammadur rasūlu 'llāh.*

This went on and on, as they continued to work, with a will and with good strong heaves. *Lā ilāha illa 'llāh* he would chant; *Muḥammadur rasūlu 'llāh* would come the vigorous response. Such a scene represents, of course, a kind of living in which a split into religious and secular has not come—or has not yet come—to segment life. At a different level, of course, are the formal ceremonies in the weekly service of some of the Islamic Sufi orders, in which the initiate devotees will induce a mystic ecstasy or trance by the solemn and rhythmic repetition or incantation of the formula.

Between these two comes a religious use such as that by the *mu'azzin* in his call to prayer five times a day, whose sonorous recitative from the minaret punctuates village or town life and summons the faithful to turn for a moment from their routine affairs to the life of the spirit.

I have called this creed a symbol; and in some ways it plays in Muslim life a role similar to that played, for instance, for Christians by the cross. Nonetheless it is not a pictorial sign but a verbal one, and this itself is significant and appropriate. The role of linguistic form, of words, in Islamic religious life is quite special. I have already spoken of the written word—calligraphy—as a typical Muslim art form. This community has carried the decorative use of writing probably further than has any other people. And take revelation itself. In the Christian case this takes the form of a person, whereas for the Muslim it too is verbal. In the Qur'an, God makes himself and His purpose known to man in the form of words. It is altogether appropriate, then, that the chief symbol of Islam should also be verbal.

So far, I have allowed myself to follow the usual Western practice of calling this two-phrase synopsis of the Muslim's faith a 'creed'. For to do this is not altogether misleading, though you will have seen that its place in Muslim life is only partly correlative with that of the creed for us. It is time now, however, to modify this still further. We need to see more carefully ways in which the faith of other people is expressed in patterns that do not quite correspond to our own—or even to what we expect of them.

In some ways, then, the 'two words' of the Islamic assertion do constitute a creed, a statement of belief, but in other ways they do not; and the Muslims do not themselves call this formula a creed. They call it, rather, a 'witness'. Regularly the statement is preceded by the words 'I bear witness that' there is no god . . . and so on. And even when these actual terms are not employed, an idea of witnessing is involved, and can be quite basic. The Islamic has been one of the three great missionary communities in human history (along with the Buddhist and the Christian); and the idea of bearing witness to his faith is quite central to a Muslim's attitudes. His assertion is not so much an affirmation of belief, as a proclamation—of conviction. And in a subtle fashion, there is involved here a point that I rather imagine is more basic in all religious life perhaps than is usually recognized. It is this: that it is not so much that the Muslim *believes* that God is one, and Muhammad is His prophet, as it is that he takes this for granted. He presupposes it, and goes on from there. From his own point of view, one might almost say that, so far as he is concerned, he *knows* that these things are so, and what he is doing is simply announcing them, bearing witness to them.

The same kind of thing is true, I think, of all religious life. One distorts a Christian's faith, for example, by saying simply that he believes Jesus Christ to be divine, to be the son of God. He would rather say that he recognizes this—these are the facts, and he has been fortunate enough to see them. In the Christian case the matter has been somewhat complicated by the use in Western languages of a single verb, *credo*, 'I believe', and so on, both for intellectual belief (belief that) and for religious faith (belief in)—though men of faith have insisted that the two things are different. Anyway, I feel that true faith has already begun to crumble a bit, if it has not actually gone, as soon as people have reduced what used to be the data, the presuppositions, of their world view to a set of true-or-false propositions—I mean, when what was once the presupposed context or intellectual background for a transcending religious faith becomes rather the foreground of intellectual belief. This is one of the fundamental troubles in the modern world, and one of the fundamental problems arising from a recognition of religious diversity—that what used to be unconscious premises become, rather, scrutinized intellectualizations. At this new level the believer himself begins to wonder if he really 'believes', in this new sense (and often enough finds that he actually does not).

In the Islamic case, as in the Jewish, the word of God is, fundamentally, an imperative. And even the proclamation of God's oneness is in some ways more a command, to worship Him alone, than merely an invitation to believe that He is there alone. Faith differs from belief in many ways, and goes beyond it; one way is that faith in God's oneness is a recognition of His unique and exclusive authority, and an active giving of oneself to it. Like the Christian, the classical Muslim theologian has seen faith as a commitment. He would understand at once St. James in the New Testament writing, 'You believe that God is one? You do well: the devils also believe—and tremble'. To a truly religious man, the question is not one merely of belief, but of doing something about it.

Having said that, however, we on the outside may still ask what the presuppositions are; what belief is presumed, for those who do go on to commitment.

We find ourselves having come round, then, to the question that we earlier postponed, the question of the meaning of the 'two words'. What does it mean to say 'There is no god but God, and Muhammad is His apostle'? What does it mean, that is, to a Muslim—to someone to whom these two clauses are not merely true, but profoundly and cosmically true, are the two most important and final truths in the world, and the most crucial for man and his destiny?

Let us look at each in turn.

To say that there is one God, and that He alone is to be worshipped, means at its most immediate, as it meant in pagan Arabia when it was first proclaimed, a rejection of polytheism and idolatry. When Muhammad captured Mecca in A.D. 630, and set up Islam in triumph, he gave a general amnesty to the human beings there who had resisted his cause and were now defeated, but he smashed without quarter the idols—three hundred and sixty of them, it is said—in the shrine of the Ka'bah, the figures of the pagans' gods. From that day to this, Islam has been uncompromising in its doctrine of monotheism, and its insistence on transcendence: God the Creator and Judge is Lord of all the universe, is high above all his creatures and beyond them, and beyond all their imaginings—and certainly beyond all their representations. Other deities, it asserts, are but the figments of men's wayward imagination, are unadulterated fiction; they just do not exist. Man must not bow down to them nor worship them, or look to them for help, or think about them. God is God alone; on this point Islam is emphatic, positive, and clear.

Historically, as the Islamic movement has spread, across the centuries, from Arabia through the Near East and into Central Asia and has penetrated China, into India and South-East Asia, across Africa and still today is spreading down into Africa, it has met polytheism in many forms, has attacked it and replaced it. Like the Church in the Roman Empire and Northern Europe, and later in the Americas, so Islam in large parts of the world has superseded polytheistic practice and thought with monotheistic.

At a subtler level, for those capable of seeing it, the doctrine has meant also at times, and certainly ought to mean, a rejection of human tyranny. God alone is to be worshipped, to be served. For the man for whom this faith is sufficiently vivid, this can mean that no earthly power, no human figure, deserves or can legitimately claim man's allegiance; and any attempt to impose a purely human yoke on man's neck is an infringement not only of human dignity but of cosmic order, and to submit to it would be sin. Admittedly there has been, especially in periods of decline, an alternative interpretation whereby God's governance of affairs is taken as determining not what ought to be but what is. This view has led to fatalism—a passive acceptance of whatever happens. Perhaps you will feel that I am intruding my own predilections here in siding with those Muslims who have taken rather the activist line, asserting God's will as something to be striven for, as was done more widely in Islam's earlier centuries, and is beginning to be done again in our own day. You will agree, in any case, that it is legitimate and proper, in interpreting other men's faith as in one's own, to try to see it at its best and highest. That at least is what I am trying to do throughout these talks.

There is still a third level of meaning, which was stressed particularly by the Sufi mystics in the mediæval period, and is beginning to get wide support today. According to this view, to worship God alone is to turn aside from false gods not only in the concrete sense of idols and religious polytheism, but also in the subtler sense of turning aside from a moral polytheism, from false values—the false gods of the heart. To pursue merely earthly goals, to value them, to give them one's allegiance and in a sense to worship them—goals such as wealth, prestige, sex, national aggrandizement, comfort, or all the other distractions and foibles of human life—this, says the sensitive Muslim conscience, like the sensitive Christian or Jewish one, is to infringe the principle of monotheism. Similarly, to look for help to purely mundane forces, to rely upon armies or clever stratagems, to trust anything that is not intrinsically good—this is to have more than one god. The affirmation that God alone is to be worshipped means, for the man of true piety and rigorous sincerity, that no other objective must claim man's effort or loyalty; he must fear no other power, honour no other prize, pursue no other goal.

I would mention, finally, one other interpretation of the 'no god but God' phrase, one that again has been put forward by some of the mystics. This one has not been widespread, even among these; yet I mention it because I personally find it attractive, and it shows the kind of thing that can be done. This particular view is in line with the general position taken by the mystics that the religious life is a process, a movement in faith. According to this interpretation, then, the statement that 'there is no god but God' is to be taken in stages. No man, this reading suggests, can legitimately and truly say 'God' who has not previously said, and meant, 'no god'. To arrive at true faith, one must first pass through a stage of unbelief. 'There is no god': this comes first, and must be lived through in all sincerity, and all terror. A person brought up in a religious tradition must have seen through that tradition, its forms and fancies, its shams and shibboleths; he must have learned the bleakness of atheism, and have experienced its meaninglessness and eventually its dread. Only such a person is able to go on, perhaps only years later, to a faith that is without superficiality and without merely cheap and second-hand glibness. If one has said 'there is no god' with the anguish of a genuine despair, one may then, with God's grace, go on to say '. . . but God', and say it with the ecstasy of genuine insight.

Let us turn, next, to the second proposition: 'Muhammad is the apostle of God'. The first thing to grasp here is that this is a statement not about Muhammad's status but about his function. The Islamic concept of apostle, or prophet, is quite special; and one is misled if one too readily assumes that this corresponds to ideas familiar to us in the West. The underlying notion here, and it is tacitly presupposed by the formulation, is that God has something to say to mankind, and has from time to time chosen certain persons in various communities through whom to say it; the assertion here is that Muhammad was one of those persons. It too, then, is in significant degree, and even primarily, a statement about God. As the theologians worked it out, it involves the conviction that God is not essentially passive, inscrutable, content to remain transcendent; rather than from all eternity, and as part of His very nature, He is the kind of God who has something to say to mankind. What He has to say is what we would call the moral law. When He created the universe and when He created man, He did not exactly create the moral law, for this comes closer to being, rather, a part of Himself—but anyway He ordained it, or set it forth, and He created man to receive it, free and responsible to carry it out.

This is the first affirmation. The second is that He communicated this moral law to mankind. He did not leave man to grope about in the dark, to discover for himself, by his own efforts, what he could. No; God Himself acted, and spoke—spoke through the mouth of the prophets and apostles, beginning with Adam, that is, from the very beginning of history. Religion is nowadays sometimes spoken of as man's search for God. On this, the Islamic position is like the Jewish and the Christian, rejecting such a view emphatically, and asserting rather that God takes the initiative. As Micah put it, in our Judæo-Christian tradition, 'He hath *shown* thee, O man, what is good . . .'. Man's business in the religious life is not a quest but a response.

Thirdly, in the message that God communicated is to be found, in the Muslim view, not what is true so much, though of course they do hold this, but what is *right*. The position differs from the Christian in that it is a revelation *from* God, more than *of* God. The apostle or prophet is one who conveys to men the message that God wants them to know; namely, how they should live. Accordingly, out of the message theoreticians and systematizers have extracted and constructed a law, finally elaborated in all detail and ultimately turned into a static system.

One last point, and with this I close. I said a moment ago that the phrase 'Muhammad is the apostle of God' is a statement not about Muhammad's status so much as about his function. Let me elaborate this just a little. The position stands over against the quite different Christian orientation, which sees the person of Christ as central and ultimate, pre-existent and divine. Muslims also posit a central and ultimate truth, pre-existent and divine, namely the Qur'an—not a person but a book, or better, what the book says. Muhammad plays in the Islamic scheme the role played in the Christian system by St. Paul or St. Peter; namely, that of an apostle who proclaims among men God's gift to them, which in the Islamic case is the scripture. In contrast to the Christian conviction, you might almost say that the Muslims' affirmation about their prophet is not a statement about Muhammad's person at all, but about the Qur'an and 'what Muhammad brought'. To say that he is an apostle, sent by God, is to affirm these things that we have noted, about God, and about the kind of universe that we live in, and about the human situation, and morality; and then within that framework it is to assert further that the message purveyed by Muhammad is authentic. If you believe this, then you are accepting as incumbent upon you in an ultimate moral sense the practical duties that flow from this tradition. For you are recognizing the obligation to perform them as not of human origin but of divine. Those of us for whom the content of morality is not defined in this historical source should nonetheless not allow this to obscure from us the cosmic things that those inspired from this source are saying about morality, about man, and about God.

CHAPTER FIVE

The Chinese

YIN-YANG CIRCLE

I N THESE INQUIRIES into the religious life of the world, we have in each case been singling out one symbol of a community's belief, and exploring it—hoping that it might serve as a rewarding clue to the religious orientation of that group. For China I have chosen the ancient *yin-yang* circle.

Unlike the symbols we have considered in our other talks, this is not a ceremony or a phrase but a pictorial design, a visual image. In some ways this facilitates our task, since we in the West are quite accustomed to the use of visual images in religious symbolism, and indeed think of this as altogether standard and appropriate. Moreover, we see perhaps more clearly with visual images than in the case of any other type of religious

67

symbol that the item is indeed a symbol, a representation pointing beyond itself, and capable of meaning different things to different people, depending on their capacity and insight and the quality of their personal life. We know that an image means more to a believer than to an outsider; much more to a profound and devout believer than the same image does or can to a lukewarm or superficial one; and indeed, that the meaning lies not in the image itself but in what the man of faith brings to it. We are not quite so trained to recognize that this sort of thing is true also of a theological system, for instance; though it, too, I personally take as a symbol, an intellectual one this time, something whose meaning lies beyond the immediate sense of its statements: the phrases in themselves mean something, but symbolize something more—as in poetry.

On the other hand, we are at a certain disadvantage in considering a visual image, since I am going simply to write about it, and of course such an image is meant not to be written about but to be looked at. It would be much more effective if all of us could have the actual *yin-yang* circle in front of our eyes throughout our discussion. Not only is it extremely simple, like any good religious symbol, whereas my verbal comments upon its meaning may become complex and elaborate. Also it is graceful, and serenely quiet. This, indeed, is part of its point; and I am afraid that my endeavours to interpret it, even if they succeed in catching something of the import, may yet lack, certainly, the simplicity and the charm.

I imagine that most of you have seen the image. Take a circle, and divide it in two equal and congruent parts by drawing an S-shaped curve from top to bottom, so that you have two as it were curved tear-drops nestling one against the other. One should be black and the other white; or, if you have colour, one red and the other black. You may if you like put a dot of white in the middle of the largest bulbous part of the black, and a black dot in the white; suggesting that each half of the circle lightly touches or invades the other. You are left with a perfectly symmetrical figure, such that you cannot say whether it is a black circle with a graceful white tear-drop in it, or a white circle with a graceful black tear-drop; or two contrasting tear-drops so interposed as to constitute together a perfect whole, flawlessly circular, or a perfect circle divided into two equal, contrasting, interpenetrating, and lovely parts.

With its total balance, and its endless, sinuous curves, it is a superb synthesis of rest and movement, of contrast and concord, of immediacy and ultimacy.

Before we go on to probe the symbolism, may I comment on a prior point? It is a Western convention to talk of the religions of the world, imagining these as so many distinct entities, each a system of its own. Within such a framework, Westerners have learned to speak of three religions in China, and to label these Confucianist, Taoist, and Buddhist. Having set up this pattern, we then break it down again by saying that a Chinese may belong to all three at once, which leaves us just a trifle perplexed. As you see, I am not following this custom. I have deliberately entitled this essay 'The Chinese', rather than using any one of the specific names of religious traditions there. Further, in order to represent the religious life of that people as typically and as faithfully as any one item could, I have chosen a symbol that is not specifically Confucian, or Taoist, or Buddhist. It has been used by all three groups, more copiously in Taoist lore perhaps than in the teaching of the other two traditions, but certainly not exclusively; and actually it is considerably more ancient in China than any of these. Its use can be traced far back into the dim past, before the rise or introduction of any one of the three great traditions, though it is now part of them all. By choosing it, then, we illustrate the essential catholicity of the religious orientation of the Chinese. And indeed, as we shall see presently, the symbol itself represents and affirms the harmonious holding together of contrasts in a balanced synthesis, the integrating of divergence into a rounded whole.

But this is to anticipate. Originally, and most immediately, the image represents *yang* and *yin*, the two fundamental principles in Chinese cosmology. *Yang* is hot, dry, active, light, and masculine; *yin* is cold, moist, passive, dark, and feminine. *Yang* is movement, *yin* is rest. The interplay of these two principles produces the five elements of fire, metal, earth, wood, and water; and these in turn in varying proportions combine to produce everything that is. Fire is almost pure *yang*, water is almost pure *yin*—almost, but not quite; for nothing exists that does not combine something of both. I have called them principles, but they have also been termed modes. And not only every substance, but also every event, is a combination of the two. Heaven is more *yang*, earth more *yin*. Man is more *yang*, woman more *yin*. Victory is more *yang*, peace more *yin*. They may also be regarded as phases, ever succeeding one another in endless revolution and in infinite variety. Night and day, summer and winter, male and female, stability and change—the universe as a whole and in all its parts, its being and its becoming, all is an expression of the underlying *yin* and *yang* in eternal interplay. There is nothing in which *yin* and *yang* do not participate.

Now this theory of *yang-yin* has been widely used in all sorts of contexts in China: as a hocus-pocus in elaborate superstitions, as a basic notion in systematic scientific thought, as an intellectual framework for brilliant and profound philosophy. It would be out of place for us here to follow up the superstition side, in line with my general policy of trying to consider religious life at its best, not at its most ordinary. So far as science is concerned, of course early Chinese thought in this realm, though historically of major world importance, has long since been superseded; but it is perhaps worth mentioning that some observers hold that twentieth-century science in the West is moving closer to a fundamental *yin-yang* type of interpretation of the natural universe than traditional Western views—I shall be returning to this, briefly, in a few minutes.

So far as Chinese philosophy goes, I shall do no more than mention the name of Chu Hsi, the twelfth-century thinker at the time of the Sung Renascence who reformulated the classical tradition of learning in China into what is now called Neo-Confucianism. His powerful and lucid system of thought lasted until our own day as the chief formulation of China's more or less national ideology. He constructed it on a basis in which the *yin-yang* idea was prominent.

But our concern is with the *yang-yin* circle as a religious symbol. And as with symbols in other traditions that we have considered, I shall not try to exhaust or even to systematize all the things that it can mean or has meant to diverse groups that have cherished it. Rather I shall simply explore some avenues that it opens up, so as to get some insight into the faith and some sympathy with the attitude of persons whose outlook has been different from that traditional with us. Indeed, we shall concentrate on one significance, since I find this basic and deeply illuminating. It is the notion of what I call complement dualism.

We in the West are familiar with another type of dualism, which we may call conflict dualism. In this, two basic forces are in collision, as opposites that struggle and clash: good and evil, right and wrong, black and white, true and false. This type of dualism seems to have its origin about the middle of the first millennium B.C. in the Tigris-Euphrates valley or in Iran. There the traditions from Zarathustra (or 'Zoroaster') formulated it into a metaphysics, a dichotomy which split the cosmos into two opposing forces led by Ahura Mazda and Angra Mainyu—or God and the Devil. In other forms, sometimes considerably modified, it found its way into the Jewish, Christian, and the Islamic traditions, and has been vigorously resuscitated in recent times on a world scale by Marxism. In our religious traditions a Devil, over against God, was long accepted; Heaven and Hell are postulated; and the saved and the damned, the sheep and the goats. In the Marxist case there is a variation on this kind of outlook; Marxism rejects metaphysics, and yet interprets this world in terms of dualist conflict: the class struggle, *bourgeoisie* and proletariat, capitalism and

communism, exploiters and exploited, thesis and antithe-
sis. In the religious and in the Marxist version, a final
unity, whether synthesis or ultimate triumph of one side,
is envisaged; but meanwhile the world is analysed in bi-
polar terms. For two and a half thousand years the Near
East and the Western worlds have either postulated or
sympathized with a cosmic conflict dualism; or, in a
dichotomy of less antagonism, with a dualism of opposition. If not God and the Devil, at least God and the
world, man and nature, matter and spirit, either/or.

India has never quite understood this, and *its* basic
orientation has been monistic. For Indians, reality is not
two, but one; and even religious assertions are thought
of not as true or false, but as more or less approximate:
the world is not black and white, but a panorama, not
of grey but of reds and greens and yellows. The difference is much more radical and more pervasive than we
usually allow, between India on this matter and the
West with its yes-or-no approach to life. The *yin-yang*
circle of China which we are at present considering
symbolizes another view, dualist, but of a dualism of a
different type; one that is, I think, radically different
from both India and the West, and is worth our trying to
understand.

Let us look at that circle once again. The light and the
dark are distinct, are in contrast; but not in conflict.
They combine to form a rounded whole. The form of
each presupposes the other. The direction of each is towards the area of the other, but as it moves both move, in
a rhythmic cycle of phased and balanced symmetry.

Let us take as one example the question of man and
nature. If you do not see what I mean by looking at

this *yang-yin* image of the circle, look instead at any typical Chinese painting, perhaps of a quiet fisherman by a waterfall where with subtle restrained suggestion and in a few incredibly delicate touches the person merges into the landscape, and the beauty lies in a sense of utter peace found in a union of man with nature. In the Western tradition there are, of course, exceptions; but certainly one of the dominant motifs has been, in contrast, that of man *against* nature—out of which has grown our ruthlessly applied technology. We regard nature if not as something against which to struggle, at least as something to subordinate and to control and to use. This is expressed in the first chapter of Genesis, where God is pictured as creating man and woman and setting them on earth and saying, 'Be fruitful and multiply, and fill the earth and subdue it; and have dominion . . .' . The *yin-yang* circle symbolizes a different mood.

Similarly, in the West the concept God is of course one of ultimate importance; whereas in China this kind of concept has not been particularly significant or much developed. This does not mean that the Chinese have been less religious than we; rather that they have been religious in a different way, and have conceptualized their faith in a different way. With us, God creates the world, out of nothing. It stands over against him; and even man, though created in God's image, is yet a creature, with God sometimes conceived as the 'wholly other'. In the *yang-yin* circle before us you might say that there is nothing to correspond to our concept of God; or alternatively, you might say that in so far as this concept signifies perfection, what corresponds is the circle itself, the whole, the symmetry and balance, the perfection of the various parts.

Again, if we take the concept *Tao,* which is in a sense ultimate reality or ultimate value for many Chinese (and not only Taoists), one thing to say about it is that it signifies the way (*Tao* means 'way') in which the *yin-yang* process operates. It has been remarked that the Chinese have always felt that the universe was quite capable of looking after itself, of functioning on its own. In so far as this signifies that it does not need a power or person outside itself to look after it and to run it, the point is valid. But the *way* in which the functioning dependably and beautifully proceeds is profoundly significant for the Chinese, is a final truth. It is, if you like, for them an object of faith. The *yang-yin* circle at which we are looking is after all a *circle*—not a jagged or chaotic mess, as the modern atheist without a faith is beginning to suspect the world is. To represent totality as an harmonious perfection in movement is no mean affirmation.

Or let us take the question of good or evil. It is not unknown in China that *yang* in this dualism has represented or been associated with good, or the good spirits, and *yin* with evil, or the demons. More basic and more representative, however, has been the view that in this symbol good is represented by the harmony of the contrasting parts. Evil would be an absence of that harmony. In this sense, and it is the dominant one, the symbol is what we might call idealist, representing the universe as it ought to be; the actual state of human affairs, things as they are, would then be represented presumably by such a circle in which the S-curve were out of proportion, or all askew or jagged. Man's immorality—of which

you may be sure the Chinese have not been unaware!—
is that which introduces distortion into the natural harmony of the world. The two halves of our symbol, then,
are not good and evil; both are good, and a further good
lies in their due proportion. Evil then is not the opposite
of good, it is the absence of good.

Our image, then, symbolizes, for instance, male or female; and to one who has meditated upon it and seen
truth through it, it is meaningless to ask whether man is
better than woman, or vice versa, and wrong to think in
terms of a conflict between them. Both are necessary;
each is defined in terms of the other; each is fulfilled in a
totality that both constitute. And evil in this realm oc-
curs if the integrity of either part, or the integrity of the
two together, is infringed. Similar considerations apply
to problems of the individual and society; of stability
and change; abiding truth and ceaseless flux.

In area after area of life, both moral and intellectual,
this image symbolizes a faith in a dualism of complement
rather than of conflict.

By faith I mean in part a way of looking at the world.
A few minutes ago we spoke of this on the intellectual
side in science, and remarked that there seemed perhaps
some justification for thinking, as some have suggested,
that the *yin-yang* symbol serves to represent an intellectual outlook that makes some sense in the scientific field.
I do not know enough science to speak here more than
very tentatively, but it does seem that in several areas
scientists have been moving away from a sharp opposi-
tion-dichotomy outlook towards one rather of the com-
plementarity of opposites. I suppose the most obvious
example is the positive and negative electric charge, each

of which is defined in terms of the other, and of which the *yang-yin* symbol would be perhaps a fairly reasonable presentation. Another instance might be the wave theory and the quantum theory of light, each of which is valid though partial, while a unified view embraces both. Even the distinction between true and false is not nearly so sharp in science as it used to be in our pre-scientific tradition: scientific measurements, for instance, are regarded, rather, as correct to a certain degree of accuracy. Other subtler dichotomies that have been losing their sharpness are those between organism and environment, which we now see as together constituting a reality; or in philosophy, take traditional issues such as freedom and determinism. This problem used to be put in such a way as to presume that an intelligent man must choose: *either* this *or* that. Nowadays one has to hold the two notions, if they are valid at all, in some different sort of mutual relation, not as clear-cut alternatives; freedom and determinism together in constant interplay constitute our life. Similarly in psychosomatic medicine and psychology: mind and body (our traditional terms) are seen as referring not to two distinct entities opposed to each other, but as two interacting components dynamically constituting a total circle. Again, science and religion themselves a century ago seemed to many people to be alternatives in bitter conflict; whereas today many feel that a truer view would see them as two different but complementary elements revolving in a larger, and dynamic, whole. It is an interesting affirmation, symbolically imaged, that of the universe as a whole or any part of it there are always two contrasting facets or modes, of which neither is complete without the other,

and of which both taken together in due balance constitute the truth.

However this may be, the more interesting and immediately relevant aspects of the matter for our purposes are the moral ones; and among these, not least
significant are the political. I think that we must not un-
derestimate the significance of the outlook that is here
involved, even for practical and immediate affairs. There
are many, many people who have no idea that their actions are influenced by metaphysical traditions which
they certainly could not themselves state, and in which
they probably do not suppose themselves to be interested; and yet such people often react to events and be-
have on most major issues in ways that in fact are related to inherited presuppositions such as those at stake
here. John Foster Dulles, it seems to me, is simply one
example of a statesman whose spontaneous and sustained
attitude to the world presupposed conflict dualism; and
many lesser men respond surprisingly readily and constantly to analyses of affairs and to proposed programmes
of action in such terms, just because they have been
brought up to see the world in terms of black and
white in conflict or opposition. I personally would be
much happier if I felt that our political leaders were
sitting down to ponder such problems as Berlin, after
having spent half an hour contemplating with some sort
of religious faith the *yin-yang* circle of balanced contrast; or (having been brought up on such a symbol
since childhood) took it for granted that ultimate truth
lies in harmony. And certainly it is a significant matter
that China has passed into the hands of rulers who, being
Marxist, would reject this internal tradition in favour

of an Armageddon-type ideology that is either/or, and reads history and plans policy in terms of clash and struggle. For them, not co-existence but conflict.

I should like to close this essay with reference to the point at which we began, that of religious diversity. The Chinese have not been unaware of contrasts between the teachings of, let us say, K'ung Fu-tse and Lao-tse, from whom the Confucianist and Taoist traditions respectively stem. As our circle symbolizes, however, they usually comprehend both within the compass of a larger whole. In the modern world some voices are suggesting that all mankind must learn to see religious diversity in this way, so that we may construct on earth an englobing concord and fellowship that recognizes differences and even contrasts in the religious realm as parts within an harmonious circle of world-wide human community —the truth lying not with one element in the complex but in the adjustment of each to the others. This is a question that we must face in our next essay. In the meantime I may remark that of course this view is opposed by those that see such a solution as a betrayal of one's own loyalties. They assert that truth is truth, and must be upheld, it must not be dissolved in camaraderie. The debate between these two could become quite sharp: between the universalist and the particularist. As I have said, we shall be returning to this problem in another connection. For the moment, however, let me relate it to our present concern, our Chinese symbol. What I myself see in the *yang-yin* symbol with regard to this matter, if I may be allowed this personal note, is not the first solution only, not merely an image that would reduce Christian truth to a part of some larger whole.

Rather, I find it a circle embracing, for Christian truth itself, both this liberal universalism and at the same time the absolutist interpretation—the two in constant interplay. Its point is to deny that one has to choose between orthodoxy and liberalism, between loyalty to one's own faith in all its fullness, and loyalty to other men's faith in all its variety. An effete and watered-down eclecticism that is substituted for Christian orthodoxy and for other men's orthodoxy is no final solution. A truly Christian attitude to outsiders must involve both the validity of Christian orthodoxy *and* an acceptance of men of other orthodoxies as one's brothers—in one's own eyes, and in the eyes of God. In this, the image says to me, as in all ultimate matters, truth lies not in an either/or, but in a both/and.

CHAPTER SIX

Christians and Jews

IN CONSIDERING 'the faith of other men', there comes a
point when one may ask, as I propose to do now, how
all this impinges on one's own faith. Or I may say here,
'on our own faith', meaning that of Christians and Jews,
since most of us here in the West who have religious
faith are in one of these two traditions. And quite major
internal issues are indeed involved for us in our relations
with men of other faith.

Now it would be possible to put forward an argument
that in a series of this kind, or in any academic endeavour, one should treat all religious traditions in what is
sometimes called an 'objective' fashion, standing outside
all of them and treating all alike. On this basis, we
should deal with the Christian and the Jewish traditions
just as we have with the Buddhist or Muslim, taking a
single item in each case and endeavouring to set forth its
meaning. Now for one thing this would be a trifle silly,
since of course you already know more about these traditions than I could tell you in half an hour, if I stuck to
sheer exposition. I feel that it will be much more rewarding if we together explore, instead, the more relevant and
more searching question of what is involved, for *our* faith,
in the recognition of the profundity of other people's.

For I believe that there is a relation between a man's own personal faith and his understanding of the religious life of other men. I think that each is relevant to the other, and that it ought to be relevant. Our objective, I submit, is not to try to make these things irrelevant, but rather to understand the relevance, to criticize it and purify it and use it. In other words, interreligious understanding is not merely an intellectual or academic or 'objective' question; it is also a religious question. To ask about other men's faith is in itself to raise important issues about one's own.

The fact of my being Christian is relevant to my understanding the faith of Hindus, Buddhists, Muslims, and the like—the fact of my being Christian, and the quality of it, the question of what kind of Christian I am, and what kind I ought to be. Relevant similarly to your understanding are the questions of whether you are Christian or Jewish or sceptic, and if so what kind of Christian or Jew or sceptic you are, and the theological and moral question of what attitude we ought properly to have, all of us, to each other; and to others across the world.

If you really insist on symmetry here, then I may concede that actually if I were proffering these essays in India, I would in that case present Christian and Jewish faiths in brief introductions, I would omit the essays that I have given here for the Hindu and Islamic traditions, and I would include instead of these a discussion of the religious implications for Hindus and Muslims of the fact that they hold their faith in a religiously plural world.

In other words, an ideally complete picture of our subject, impartially valid for the whole world, would include two sets of things: first, an exposition of each faith as it looks, or can at its best look, to an outsider; second, a consideration, from within each faith, of the fact of mankind's religious diversity, and its internal implications for that faith.

Because I am writing in the West, I have chosen to do the expository presentation only for those traditions unfamiliar in our community; and to consider the internal implications, in this essay, only for those established here.

I shall return towards the end of this present discussion to saying something explicitly about Jews. In the meantime, I intend to talk in general, or as a Christian about Christians. Yet I am hoping that others among you may be able to recognize that this apparent partiality is external only. At this stage of our consideration I do not wish to preach a Christian sermon to Jews! Afterwards I shall suggest the internal application of my argument to the Jewish and other communities. Ideally the intellectually valid goal is not some cold and impersonal 'objectivity', but a self-analysis that is honest and leads to action.

Let us look, then, at three ways in which my being a Christian is involved in my awareness of other men's faith, and vice versa. We may call these three respectively that of personal experience, that of theological doctrine, and that of moral imperative. All three, we shall observe, are dynamic.

In the matter of personal experience, there is first of

all the quite straightforward point that all learning is related to previous understanding, and is an extension of it. When I learn that Muslims worship God, or fear a Day of Judgement, or affirm Creation, and so on, then my capacity to grasp what they are talking about is obviously related in part to my own prior notion of what these terms mean. Similarly your capacity to understand what a Muslim feels and thinks and experiences in his orientation to God turns in part on your own feeling and thinking and experiencing. If you are atheist or indifferent, if the idea of God leaves you totally cold or you find it repulsive, then it will be quite an extraordinary feat of sympathetic imagination if you can nonetheless enter validly into the experience of the Muslim; whereas those of us whose immediate awareness of God's presence is vivid can much more readily appreciate what the devout Muslim is talking about when he speaks of living in that presence also. I am supposing here, of course, that we are not curtailed from this appreciation by some dogmatic bond that inhibits us from extending our awareness to other people. I will come to this question presently, under our second heading of doctrinal considerations. For the moment, I am simply asserting the basic point that my capacity to apprehend significantly and truly the religious stand of other men turns in part on the understanding that I bring to it—the religious understanding: my own ability to see more in life than its material or tangible forms, my own faith in moral and spiritual realities, my own sense of the divine—in a word, my own Christian faith.

Now having said that, and emphasized it, I must nevertheless go on at once to recognize two subtleties that complicate this situation. In a sense they are obvious enough, but the final implications are certainly subtle. I said that these things are dynamic, and certainly we are pushed into deeper and deeper waters by any serious consideration here. We are never left to stand still with any simple solution; rather each person finds himself being led further and further into—into what? I was going to say 'mystery', but only the religious among you will understand what I mean. Into transcendence? That term, too, may be puzzling. Let us simply say that the further one explores, the more one discovers there is to explore. This is part of what religious life is all about, of course.

Anyway, the first of my two subtleties is that, besides similarities, there are also, naturally, differences. The first step that a Christian or a Jew must take if he is to understand Muslims is to recognize that when the Muslim speaks of 'God' or 'Judgement' or 'Creation' or the like he is talking about the same things as those to which a Christian also refers. (It is surprising how many Christians have not yet taken this first step.) Yet the second step is to discover that he is talking and thinking about them in a different way. Just how different, it is curiously difficult to say. All scholars are aware of divergences, certainly, but there is much less agreement among those scholars than you might suppose, as to just what those divergences are. It so happens that some of my own recent publications have been attempts to clarify more precisely than has been previously done the areas of correlation and lack of correlation between

Christian and Muslim religious ideas[1]. Anyway, there is certainly a task of gradually coming to recognize how men in differing traditions see things similarly, and another task of gradually coming to recognize how they see things differently.

But there is another subtlety here. First, I believe in God. A Muslim believes in God. This brings us together. Secondly, my idea of God and a Muslim's idea of God differ. This sets us apart again. But thirdly, because I am Christian, I know that God is greater—much greater—than *my* idea of Him. The Muslim, as a Muslim, knows that God is greater—much greater—than *his* idea of Him. Does this bring us together again? It may, and it may not; this depends on many things, chiefly on him and on me—and on what kind of Christian I am, and on what I do about it, and so on, and so on. As I said, this business is not static but dynamic.

I have spoken of the Islamic case, because at the immediate or basic level the similarities there with the Judæo-Christian are clearest—though it does not follow that the ultimate liaison there is strongest. Let us turn to a more conspicuous example of divergence at the basic level—say with China. I have tried, by using the *yin-yang* symbol, to show you that a man who in our sense does not believe in God may nonetheless have a faith in the universe that I personally recognize as comparable in part to my own Christian faith in God. Ultimately, the concept 'God' also is a symbol. It is one that we in

[1] See, for instance, my 'Some Similarities and Differences between Christianity and Islam. An Essay in Comparative Religion', in *The World of Islam: Studies in Honour of Philip K. Hitti*, ed. J. Kritzeck and R. B. Winder (London: Macmillan; New York: St. Martin's Press, 1959), pp. 47-59.

the West use religiously, and so do many other religious men. Yet not all religious men use it. I do not know how successful I may have been in leading you to recognize how it may be possible for a Chinese to see what I would call (though he would not) a divine quality in the universe, without his conceptualizing this in theistic terms. It is possible for him to see this, and to nourish his capacity to see it; to have faith, and to grow in faith.

Now I claim that I am able to grasp and appreciate his insight here—not easily, certainly, because it took me a long while to arrive at this, but eventually—because I, too, see this quality in the universe; and I have been led to see it by being Christian. Those of you who have also seen it in the Chinese symbol may have seen it for the first time there; but I should rather guess that most of you would have managed to grasp what I was talking about, and what the Chinese was thinking and feeling, if you yourselves had already come to this awareness of ultimate harmony and reliability and beauty in things, through a prior faith of your own.

One of the things needed in a comparative study of religion is an ability to see the divine, which I call faith. Another is an ability to see it in new and different ways.

Now this brings us to my second subtlety; which is that seeing things in a new way can sometimes mean seeing them more clearly, more deeply. I have argued that insight here involves the religious capacity that one brings to it. It may involve also a heightened religious capacity which one may bring away from it. Again, we are in dynamism. All true religious life is a process, of the enlarging and strengthening of one's faith. As a Christian, I spend my life finding more and more depth, greater and greater riches, in my Christian faith—or, put more accurately, in God, through my Christian faith.

For in that *yang-yin* symbol I hoped to show you not only something that Chinese see in the universe, but something that is actually there. The truth, if truth it is, is not in the symbol, but in the universe itself. The symbol merely expresses it. If there is any truth in the Buddhist tradition, then its truth is not 'in Buddhism', it is in the nature of things. The Buddhist tradition simply calls attention to it. It may call more or less successfully, and I as a Christian may see it or I may not; but if I do see it, and if it really is true, then I see it as a Christian, and rejoice. If anything at all is true, then it is part of God—the God whom I as a Christian worship. Truth is God. I have already been introduced to God in my Christian faith. To be introduced is probably the most profound thing in anyone's life; the most crucial. Yet it is not enough only to have been introduced; and my Christian life consists in my allowing God to make more and more of that introduction, turning it from the incipient thing it once was into the richer thing it is today, and the still richer that, I hope, He may make it become tomorrow. My faith in God is nourished through many things—the formulae of Einstein, the music of Beethoven, the surge of the sea at dawn, the communion service at my church, the theology of Aquinas, the death of my friend. By seeing these things as a Christian, I see them more truly, more richly, than I otherwise would. But also, by my seeing them, my Christian faith becomes more true, more rich, than it would otherwise be.

The same applies to my study of other men's faith.

I may illustrate the point from my study of the Muslim mystics. While studying the Persian language I was introduced to the Persian mystical poets, whose work happens to be some of the most magnificent poetry the human race has produced, and also some of the most superb expressions of mysticism. I found it immensely exciting, relevant, revealing. By reading these Muslim poets, I learned a great deal about the world, about God, about myself. I also came to understand for the first time the mystical strand in the Christian Church, which until then had been a closed book to me. Now you may feel that it was perverse of me to go this roundabout way to learn something that was in my own tradition all along. Maybe. Anyway, the fact is that I did. It may be urged that I need not, or even that I ought not, to have learned religious truth from others that I could have learned at home. My own view, and that of my more charitable Christian friends, is simply to be glad that I did learn it, and that my Christian faith is now that much deeper, richer, truer.

Perhaps it will be interesting to add, too, that it was from my study of Hindus, and of the Taoists of China, that I have learned most clearly the limitations and dangers of mysticism. Or to take another example from the other side of the arena, my Calvinist background has certainly helped me to understand and appreciate the more rigid Islamic theologians; but in turn, my study of these has illuminated for me, and helped me greatly to understand, the conservative Christian thinker Karl Barth, the power of whose position I have only lately come to appreciate.

It may be objected that other Christians have understood and appreciated Barth without having been led to it by orientalist routes. Of course this is true, and proves the very point that I am trying to make; namely, that one may arrive at an understanding of truth by various paths. This includes Christian truths. The influence on contemporary Christian theology of the modern Jewish thinker Martin Buber is also relevant here.

We come now to the second of my three levels at which one's own faith is relevant to one's understanding of other men's. This is the theological. The situation is less happy here, but also simpler.

At the first level, that of personal experience, I have naturally drawn my illustrations from the Christian orbit, not the Jewish, but those of you who are Jewish can readily enough make your own applications. Somewhat the same applies at this second level, in the theological realm, though perhaps not quite so readily. Anyway, I will speak of Christian theology. Now the fact is, as many of you know, that the dominant tradition in Christian theology has tended to take the line that other men's faith is, without discussion, false; that in other religious traditions outside the Christian, or outside the Jewish and Christian, you have men seeking God, which they are incapable of doing successfully, while only in our own do you have God seeking men, revealing and giving Himself—so that religious truth and true faith are exclusively here. This has not been the only Christian view; from the time of the early Church Fathers, most notably Clement of Alexandria, and ever since, a more liberal strand has been developed. However, the exclusivist one has, certainly, tended to dominate.

Now this is obviously relevant to the question of a Christian's understanding the faith of other men. For if he takes this theological current seriously, then he comes to the task prejudiced, in the literal sense of having made up his mind before he begins his study as to what he is going to find. Sometimes he has made it up very firmly indeed, even to the disastrous point of feeling his own faith threatened if he finds other men's faith more valid and real and true and deep than the theologians had told him it would be. The theological problem is serious —let there be no doubt about that. But here, too, the situation is dynamic. The truth may lie in the future, not the past.

The important point here is to grasp what theology is. Theology is not faith; it is the attempt on the part of the theologian, who is quite human, to give an intellectual statement for his faith. As Archbishop Temple put it, his business is to formulate in words the revelation that God has given, much as a music critic may try to express in words his appreciation of great music. The theologian in addition endeavours to relate his intellectual construction to his awareness of other relevant facts.

Now my own view here is basically quite simple; namely, that the Church has as yet not produced an adequate theology in the field of relations with other men. Christian theories of comparative religion (and for that matter other theories of comparative religion, too) have not yet been satisfactorily worked out. In the Church in earlier centuries this was attempted by men who simply did not know, and certainly did not understand, the faith of the other great religious traditions of mankind. To be quite frank, they often just did not know what they were talking about. A revision of their views is therefore necessary. I affirm, with serious conviction, that a new and truer Christian theology in this matter is today needed, and is today possible—a theology that will be truer, because more truly Christian. I am also reasonably confident that it will, in fact, be forthcoming; though I admit the matter is urgent, and I could wish more theologians were tackling the problem than is actually the case.

One simple point is that on the whole there has been a tendency to hold that, the Christian faith being true, it must follow logically that other faiths are therefore false. This logic is simply not cogent. It has done a lot of mischief, but it will not survive much longer.

The fallacy stems from confusing faith with theology, in one or other of its various forms. Since the conclusion conflicts with the faith itself, I infer that the theology used as premise must misrepresent its own master. I predict that a time will come, perhaps fairly soon, when men will see rather that if the Christian revelation is valid, then it follows from this very fact that other men's faith is genuine, is the form through which God encounters those other men, and saves them.

This is not the place to develop this argument. It is a large and serious business to elaborate a theological system that will do justice simultaneously to the facts of Christian faith and to those of the faith of other men. It is the task of those of us who have seen and felt these two to construct such an intellectual position; or to enable others in the Church to see them, so that they may develop it. This much I can say: that although there is within the Church the strong traditional bias against such an interpretation, there is also within it today, at least on this continent, a much greater readiness for such a lead than I, at least, used to imagine. My own experience, in a few attempts to put forward something in this connection, has been that a great many Christians are waiting for newness here; that they very much want to combine with their Christian faith an appreciation of outsiders', though they do not know quite how to do it. I do not here plunge into the theological argument; I simply insist that the problem is there, and is important. And I believe that when an intellectual solution is found, it will be adopted.

Finally, there is the third level of interrelation, which is the moral. It is a major misfortune that this has at times been given less consideration than the theological. Certainly it is no less important, and no less relevant. In fact, moral considerations are relevant to theology itself. It is the clear moral imperative within Christian faith that I, personally, see as providing the basis for a revised theological position, which I advocated a moment ago.

For there is no question but that morally the Christian imperative is towards brotherhood, concord, fellowship, reconciliation, and love. The starting point of Christian faith is the recognition of God in Christ. From this, two orders of inference flow: one at the intellectual level, of ideas and concepts; one at the moral level, of personal relations and action. Now we have tended to construct our systems of ideas, our theological doctrines, in such a way as to dig a great cosmic gulf between ourselves and other men—the saved and the damned. And when we have acted in terms of this dichotomy, we have at times fallen into such appalling crimes as anti-Semitism, apartheid, and the whole sorry business of colour prejudice and Western arrogance towards the outsider that underlies the profound resentments of anti-colonialism. Morally, on the other hand, our ideal has been to bridge gulfs, not to dig them; to approach all men with humility, to treat them in love and service and with total respect, and to strive for harmony and equality, and a universally human brotherhood. When we have acted in this spirit, we have done some commendable and important things.

As I see it, this conflict between our theology and our ethics has never been resolved. If one had to choose, I personally would choose the moral dimension of Christian faith; for I feel that of the two, it is the more truly Christian. Yet I am a theologian, and am not willing to acquiesce in a conflict. I feel that the Church must strive to formulate a doctrinal position with regard to men of other faith that will do more justice to our original revelation, and be more consonant with its own moral implications.

That, however, is in a sense an internal Christian question. Whatever you may think of it, there is still the point that the faith of other men involves Christians morally in two ways. First, we are morally impelled, by being Christian, to try to appreciate that faith. Let us not fool ourselves into thinking that we can love a Hindu or a Hottentot if we refuse to take seriously what is his most precious possession, his faith, and if we are supercilious about the tradition through which he finds and nourishes it. Some have suggested that it is not Christian to be as sympathetic to other men's faith as I have tried to be in these essays. I would contend rather that it is not Christian to be unsympathetic (though the Church has often enough been so). Other men might disdain outsiders' religious faith, but a Christian has no business doing so.

Secondly, we are morally impelled, by being Christian, to strive to construct a world of reconciliation and peace, of mutual understanding and global community, of universal human dignity. This means that it is our job as Christians to promote goodwill among religious communities; to create concord within religious diversity, to bridge the gulfs that so desperately separate men of differing faith. If one is honest, to accept human brotherhood as an ideal is to accept as an ideal, and to work for, a brotherhood in which some of us are Hindus, some of us are Buddhists, some of us are Muslims, some of us are Jews, some of us are Christians.

Now I come, finally, to a point that those of you who are not Christians may have awaited impatiently. I have been talking about Christian involvement; what about Jewish? What about that of secularists? The topic announced was the implications of other men's faith for Jews and Christians. Now in one sense, clearly I am not in a position to speak for Jewish implications as I have for Christian. But on this moral level I do have something to say, which is both all that I have a right to say and all that I need to say. It is this. As I have tried to elaborate, a Christian ought to feel that the Christian community, as Christian, is impelled by the moral imperative of its faith to strive for understanding and love among all men. Christians might even believe that they as Christians have greater cause, and greater resources, to strive for this than does any other group. But those of you who are Jewish will hardly be disposed to agree with this. In your case it is your Jewish faith that is your reason for so striving. Let us not quarrel as to which of us has the truer push towards universal brotherhood. We Christians on our side at least have too much for which we must ask to be forgiven. But if any of us in either community, or if anyone in any community, believes that that community is the one to bring peace among men, let them not argue the point but silently work to demonstrate this in practice.

The same applies to Buddhists and to all men. What a marvellously new day would have dawned, if the only rivalry among religious communities were a competition as to which could make the greatest contribution to mutual concord!

My own prayer would be that we should not compete in this but learn, somehow, out of loyalty each to our own vision, to collaborate in it.

CHAPTER SEVEN

Conclusion

I N THIS FINAL CHAPTER, can we stand back and in some
fashion consider the total picture? Can we ask: what
emerges from the fact of mankind's religious diversity
itself? What inferences in general may one draw?

Now one possible way to go at this sort of question
would be the intellectualist or theoretical, addressing
oneself to such important issues as how to conceptualize
faith itself, in the light of its multiformity: not the faith
of this group or that, but religious faith in general. How
can one characterize it, what sort of quality in man can it
be said to be, in a way that will do justice to our own
and to other men's? Attempts at definition have been
made in the past, by philosophers of religion and by
theologians, and also by other observers more externalist,
in fields such as sociology and psychology; yet often
these proffered definitions have been on the basis of
only limited material, chiefly that of one particular tradition, or alternatively with what some of us who do
have faith feel is only limited insight into the quality of
what it is in which we are involved. There is, I think, a
legitimate and serious task here for the comparative re-
ligionist, to formulate ideas that attempt to do justice to
both the profundity and the diversity—in the hopes of

constructing theories that would prove acceptable both to Jews and to Buddhists, both to Muslims and to Christians, as well as being cogent within the academic tradition. This is an exciting and important endeavour; a pioneering one, because it is only in its infancy, but promising.

Now I myself have developed certain views in this realm, and I wondered for a time whether the function of this essay might be for me to air them; but I have decided against this for two reasons. The first is that they are tentative and untried, and I do not feel that this would be a proper occasion to propound speculative theories, which, however suggestive or even illuminating they might or might not be, are essentially hypotheses. My chief concern is not to push my own views but to take the opportunity to insist that the problems are significant—and soluble; and to urge more people to take them up. The theoretical aspect of these studies is important. We need more university departments, more books, more minds at work in this area of inquiry, more research, more scholarship, more creative thinking.

My second reason for moving on is a still more persuasive one. It is the vivid recognition that the question is not only theoretical and intellectualist. The massive dimension of the issue is the historical, the practical: and it is about this that I wish to speak now. We need new ideas, certainly, that will allow us to live in this new phase of human history into which we are moving, without blundering in bewildered confusion or narrow blindness. But rather than discuss the ideas that might serve, let us give our attention rather to the actual facts of our modern situation, the emerging condition of our life on earth in the face of which not only new ideas but a new will and a constructive effort are demanded of us. It is not the failure to solve the problem theoretically that threatens us, so much as a failure to recognize that the problem is there, and is serious. The basic question of comparative religion in the modern world is not solely an intellectual question, requiring some neat theoretical formula—those of us who are theoreticians can handle that, at least if enough good men will join in the search. No; the basic question here is an historical one and is a question for all men—large, urgent, and deeply involving us every one. It is a matter most of all for our statesmen, to lead; but for all of us to participate.

I call it an historical question because it is a matter of what is actually going on in our century in world affairs, and of the direction in which civilization is to move, and of our capacity to enter a new phase of human history. It is a question of our recognizing new trends and new goals, and of our constructing here on earth over the next hundred years or perhaps less the new kind of world that alone can be viable today.

The title of this essay is 'Conclusion'; but I hope that no one of you will have taken that too seriously. For the religious life of mankind is not yet over. Indeed there are some facets of it that in a sense are just beginning, at least on a world scale—the very facets that most concern us here. Whatever a man may think regarding his own system, it is conspicuously clear to every observer that the religious traditions of other men are manifestly in continuing development. Even more striking is that the relations among religious groups are today in profound and even rapid evolution. The total religious history of mankind is entering a new phase.

For one thing, it is a rather new development that a man should be seriously asked to understand a religious tradition other than his own. What will develop when this becomes general it would be interesting to be able to predict. More radical, it is a new thing that a man should be asked to participate in the processes of a religious tradition other than his own; and yet today it is hardly too fanciful to hold that our one-worldedness is bringing all mankind together in such a way that everyone of us is being caught up in the processes of all. We must learn to work together, all of us, in jointly constructing and jointly operating the kind of world that all of us can jointly judge worth while.

As we all know, human development has reached a point where we must construct some kind of world order, or we perish. And man being what he is, this world order must have intellectual and moral dimensions, as well as economic and political. Our vision and our loyalties, as well as our aircraft, must circle the globe.

The West, by and large, has not yet seen this problem, and hence is proving to a serious degree inept in its attempts so far towards world leadership. Westerners usually assume without question that the new world order that is struggling to be born will in basic essentials be of a Western pattern, will or even shall conform to our presuppositions, our norms, our notions of what can be taken for granted. We must wake up to the fact that the restlessness and drive of Afro-Asian 'anti-colonialism' is not merely a rejection of Western political domination, but also and increasingly a refusal to think in Western terms. We must learn to share a planet, in ever more intimate collaboration, with men who judge differently from us, who value differently, who presuppose differently—in a word, with men of different faith.

Some of you will perhaps say that surely we can get on with the business of political structures, of economic planning, of technical advance, of strategic defence, without raising extraneous issues of religious faith or cultural convictions—issues that may be interesting in themselves, but are irrelevant to secular concerns. At least I hope that some of you will feel this, because it illustrates the very point I wish to make. This division of life into two spheres, religious and secular, is a characteristically Western pattern. We tend to assume that everyone else will share it, or if they have not done so in the past then they will 'of course' learn it as they become modern. This is what I mean when I speak of our assuming that other people are like us, or that they will or must become like us tomorrow: that the problem of building a new world order is that of imposing Western civilization on the world.

This is resented, and it will not work.

People of other civilizations have not only found or cast their faith in a different form from ours. They have also related that form, their religious tradition, to their civilization differently from us. Not only does religious faith vary, but the role of religious faith in society varies in various civilizations. I have often been struck by the fact that Western culture has two fundamental sources, which it has never entirely fused: one from Greece and Rome, one from Palestine. These two traditions have sometimes been in conflict, sometimes in harmony; sometimes one has tended to dominate, sometimes the other; often the two have intertwined; but they have never coalesced. A Westerner has two loyalties: one to his religious faith; the other to his secular heritage with all its range from politics and law to grammar. In the Western world, accordingly, what the West calls 'religion' is seen as one factor in the total civilization.

In this matter, Western culture is unusual. In some cases one might almost say that a Westerner has two faiths: his religious faith, and a faith in democracy, or in his national society, or even in his civilization itself. In the case of China, India, and Islam, religious faith has not in anything like so neat a fashion been something separable from the rest of the social and cultural pattern. Although I would not like to try to define the matter precisely in a sentence or two, nonetheless one might perhaps suggest that it has not been one factor along with other factors such as the economic, the political, and so on, as in our society. It is not one element in a civilization; rather, it has been the form of that civilization. Ideally, it has been the pattern of whatever meaning the other factors in social life have. Thus in some ways one could perhaps say that it is the Western way of life that is our counterpart. This, too, is not one item in our social life; it is the form in which the items cohere. Rather than speaking of Hinduism, Buddhism, and the like, one should speak, and think, rather of the Indian way of life, the Chinese way of life, in South-East Asia the Buddhist way of life, and so on, as counterparts to the Western way of life. At the same time the faith of these men is the counterpart also, of course, of our religious faith; and the greatness of their cultural achievements in the past has had to do with their ability to integrate these two.

Now the significance of all this for our purposes here is this. Men in the Orient are not willing to set aside, or to leave out of consideration, their religious and cultural values, the form and pattern of their faith, in their resurgence in the modern world. To them, freedom and independence, which they have struggled so hard to achieve and are just now beginning to enjoy, mean in part an opportunity to reaffirm their religious and cultural traditions, to rehabilitate and revitalize and carry forward their respective ways of life. This means that the new world community towards which we hope that mankind is moving must be a world community that includes and affirms reactivated Buddhist, Hindu, and Islamic religious traditions.

What is the West going to do about this? Its first task, I would suggest, is to recognize that the question of what it is going to do about it is significant, and must be answered. In the past, civilizations have lived either in isolation from each other, or in conflict with each other. It is a novel demand that they should learn to collaborate. None of us has learned it yet; the trouble in the West is that we have hardly even recognized yet that we have to learn it. There has been some recognition, though belated and partial, that the nineteenth-century solution of Western domination by force must be abandoned. And there has begun to be a retreat from the arrogance of cultural superiority. But a constructive recognition that we positively want cultural co-operation is a step that the West has yet to take.

I have argued that the Christian Church, for instance, will have to revise its theological assertion that would divide mankind into two groups, ourselves who are saved and the rest of the world who are damned. This is an immense demand to make upon the Church, but I make it. I make an equally large demand upon our secularist society, and am somewhat less confident that it will rise to the challenge, will have the courage and vision and faith to respond. For almost equally inadequate has been the uncultural or anti-cultural attitude, of so-called 're-alism', widely adopted in the modern West, that would disregard other men's religious faith and cultural values, and would take into serious account only material things. This view is pretty well embodied in official Western policy, which spends much time and energy and money on economic assistance, but pays virtually no attention to intangibles—not by inadvertence, but by deliberate policy. In the Orient the charge is widespread, and ironically enough is fostered also by the Communists, that the West is materialistic, that we have nothing to offer but technology, that we are aware of and are concerned with differences in standard of living but not differences in cultural orientation, in philosophies, in faith; that we are fundamentally uninterested in how other people feel and how they think and what they cherish.

In other words, the Orient until now has been approached by the West chiefly on two levels—a religious level, on which the official Christian view has been that the beliefs and values of the Orient are wrong; and a secular level, in which the official view has been, and remains today, that their beliefs and values do not matter.

The fact is that to the men concerned these beliefs and values matter a very great deal. They matter not only in the sense that their adherent cherishes them, regarding them as supremely precious. More subtly and elementally, he thinks by means of them, feels in terms of them, and acts by them, and for them, and through them—even when he is thinking, feeling, and acting in the matters that we regard as political and economic.

It is my hope that these essays have helped, of course only in a minor and very introductory way, but still it is my hope that they may have helped to enable you to see men of other faith as genuine persons, with genuine faith. For that, of course, is what they are: men and women like ourselves, who see the universe that we see, but see it in different ways; and who are our neighbours. A plea to understand them as persons, then, is a plea to learn who it is with whom we are now to co-operate, with what sort of men and women we are called upon now to build jointly a jointly satisfactory world. The first step, not yet seriously taken, is to recognize that we have to learn. We have assumed far too glibly that in our relations with Afro-Asia all we have to do is to give and to teach. The Canadian government in the Colombo Plan spends fifty million dollars a year in economic assistance and technical training. When it is suggested that along with this we should spend at least half of one per cent of all such amounts on cultural interchange, so far this idea has not only not been accepted, it has not been understood—it is thought of as a frill if not a distraction, rather than as a serious and even necessary move in international affairs.

A man of faith is a man whose vision goes beyond his

immediate environment, but whose life is lived within it; so that his task, as a man of faith, is to apply that vision to the immediate environment, in all its specific actuality. The problem of the economic development of a country like Pakistan, to take one example, is partly a technical problem in economics, and is partly a question of Pakistanis' working at and in that economic development with the resolution and courage and aspiration and integrity and drive and sense of commitment and of meaning and of ease that are questions of faith. One cannot turn a poor country into a prosperous one without dams and steel-mills and hydro-electric power; but also one cannot turn a poor country into a prosperous one without getting up early in the morning, and passing up bribes, and throwing oneself into the task of implementing a vision whose benefits will accrue perhaps to posterity but not to oneself; without a loyalty to one's community and a commitment to its ideals that involve one's sense of life's meaning. Pakistan will not flourish if its citizens do not feel that life has meaning. If for them it does have meaning, then their name for that meaning is Islam.

The civilizations of the Orient are resurgent, in a new self-affirmation; and aim at a rehabilitation of their own traditions—modernized, creative, perhaps transformed, but still their own. It is their faith that life is worth living in the new and open world of today and tomorrow in the form of modernity interpreted in terms that they can understand and find good. Like us, they may fail before the challenge of modern technology, with its perplexing threat to the human spirit; or like us they may succeed. But if they do succeed, it will be in continuity from their own past, in their own self-interpretation.

The kind of world in which they and others will have managed to succeed, if they do, is one of multicultural values, of religious pluralism in tight collaboration.

I return to my question: what is the West going to do about this? There is absolutely no hope for Western leadership in the coming phase of world history unless the West can provide leadership towards that kind of world goal. Unfortunately, we have not begun to do this. Indeed, what we have begun to do gives the impression all too often that we are leading away from it. Basically, Western policy vis-à-vis the Orient, and Africa, and South America, seems to be postulated on an attempt to contrive ways of winning these people and nations over 'to our side'. Therefore we seem to them a threat to their own cultures, their own faith.

We should not ask other men to line up on our side, but we should contrive to let them see that we are on their side. This means that we must be striving to build a world in which their way of life will flourish. Ultimately this is true even of Communists—we cannot destroy Communist society, and should not wish to; we must aim at curbing it and modifying it, must aim at a new kind of world in which a transformed Communist order is integrated in a world with the rest of us. In the meantime, however, all the rest of the world is threatened today with a destructive expansion of the Communist threat. The West must realize that a global defence against this is not a defence of 'our' way of life, the Western, and not even a defence of 'freedom' in the abstract; rather, it is a defence of the Western way of life and of the Islamic way of life, and of the Indian way of life, and the Buddhist way of life, and so on.

Any man, any government, any policy that aspires to leadership in the world today must come to understand and to appreciate other men's problems and aspirations, their convictions and hopes; and must attain a point of obviously wishing to see those problems solved as well as one's own, and to see those other cultures as well as one's own survive and flourish. Only with a West that believes Oriental civilizations worth defending, and Oriental dreams worth realizing, will the Orient in general be willing to co-operate.

The new world that is waiting to be born is a world of cultural pluralism, of diverse faith. No wonder we cannot bring it to birth as long as we have not recognized this, and have not deliberately and joyously set our face in this direction.

For there are two aspects of this problem of bringing to birth tomorrow's world. One is this that we have just discussed: that of recognizing the kind of world that it will be. The other is that of willing that kind of community. Western leadership may come eventually to recognize, through the failure of other approaches, that one cannot buy friends, and cannot even make friends with persons or communities if one disdains or ignores what those persons or those communities most deeply cherish or most instinctively presume, what they take for granted and what they reach out towards. However, even a radical shift in policy to take more seriously the human side of our relations with other men will not succeed if it is done insincerely, on a purely utilitarian kind of thinking that we must take more interest in Buddhist art or Hindu philosophy or Islamic law if we are to work together with those to whom these things are precious—as a kind of more subtle method of winning them over to our side. Insincerity can cause as much resentment as disregard or disparagement. We must genuinely be on their side, not merely pretend to be. We cannot join with them in the defence of their ways of life unless we make it clear that we feel—and that means, unless we actually do feel —that those ways of life are worth defending, and are included in our long-range purpose. This was part of what I meant in saying that the problems of comparative religion involve not only an appreciation of others' faith, but also a widening and deepening of one's own.

Let no one imagine that building the new world community will be easy. Let no one imagine, either, that it must make room for the faith of Hindus, Buddhists, Muslims, and others, but not make room for ours. The Christian faith and the Jewish faith must be included in it, and even the Western secularist faith; so far as we are concerned here, as foundations of it, and as foundations of our willingness, indeed our drive, to bring it into being. Nothing less will suffice. As I said about the *yin-yang* symbol, the truth at which we are aiming must not be bought at the price of sacrificing our own loyalties, our own tradition. At such a price it would not be true, apart from the fact that at such a price there would not be men to build it. We must move forward, not back. We must envisage other men of faith moving forward, not back. It is a creative task that is demanded of us, not a destructive one of sloughing off any part of each man's vision that other men do not share.

Is this possible? Can such a variegated and yet harmonious world community be constructed? And can the men be found to construct it, by starting where they now are, each with his own faith?

I do not know. Theoretically, I am profoundly convinced that it is possible. Whether it is practically possible, in the perhaps short time within which we must achieve it, I do not know. This is a fundamental challenge facing mankind today; whether mankind will rise to it or not remains to be seen. My own faith is that it can be achieved, and is worth achieving; and while I do not know whether men will rise to it, it is my faith that they can rise to it. This is all that practically matters, for a man for whom such a faith is vivid.

Because our faith in it, and in the God who gives it validity, is fresh and simple, we are not discouraged by the possibility of failure, but rather excited by the possibility and need of success.

This excitement is real, and on that note I will close. I have spoken of these issues in comparative religion as problems, and of the tasks of envisaging and striving for a community in diversity as difficult and involving also problems. Perhaps the word 'problem' was ill chosen. They certainly are that in the sense that our best minds will only with difficulty unravel the intricacies intellectually, and only our best endeavours will carry us forward in practice. Nonetheless, certainly one should not speak as though the difficulties were depressing, or the massive nature of the practical task were anything but an exhilarating challenge. I have tried to delineate something of the dimensions of the task, and something of its immense importance. To be involved in a large and important movement, pioneering, historically crucial, with vast new issues at stake, involving the highest ideals of all mankind through history on the one hand, and the most delicate, realistic, and practical international problems of men today on the other—all this is stirring. Those who are reaching for the stars these days in the literal sense are, surely, launched on an exciting endeavour; but a metaphorical reaching for the stars that is involved in this quest for world brotherhood is more exciting, more significant, more rewarding.

PART TWO

*The Christian in a Religiously
Plural World*

This lecture was delivered before a joint meeting
of the Canadian Theological Society,
the Canadian Society of Church History,
and the Canadian Society of Biblical Studies,
held in Montreal on May 18, 1961.

W E LIVE, if I may coin a phrase, in a time of transition. The observation is a platitude; but the transitions themselves through which we are moving, the radical transformations in which we find ourselves involved, are far from hackneyed. Rather, there is excitement and at times almost terror in the newnesses to which all our cherished past is giving way. In area after area we are becoming conscious of being participants in a process, where we thought we were carriers of a pattern.

I wish to attempt to discern and to delineate something at least of the momentous current that, if I mistake not, has begun to flow around and through the Christian Church. It is a current which, although we are only beginning to be aware of it, is about to become a flood that could sweep us quite away unless we can through greatly increased consciousness of its force and direction learn to swim in its special and mighty surge.

I refer to the movement that, had the word 'ecumenical' not been appropriated lately to designate rather an internal development within the on-going Church, might well have been called by that name, in its literal meaning of a world-wide humanity. I mean the emergence of a true cosmopolitanism, or according to the wording of my title, the Christian Church in a religiously plural world, which of course is the only world there is. Like the other, *the* 'ecumenical' movement, this transformation, too, begins at the frontier, on the mission field, the active confrontation of the Church with mankind's other faiths, other religious traditions. We shall begin there, too, but shall presently see that the issues raised cannot be left out there in the distance. They penetrate back into the scholar's study, and pursue us into what we were brought up to think of as the most intimate and most sanctified recesses of our theological traditions.

Regarding the missionary movement itself, I shall begin by stating quite bluntly and quite vigorously: the missionary enterprise is in profound and fundamental crisis. There has been some temptation to recognize this more on the practical than on the theoretical level. There has been some temptation, perhaps, even not to recognize it at all! —or at least, not to recognize how serious, and how far-reaching, it is: that the whole Church is involved, and not merely 'those interested in missions'.

At the practical level the situation is acute enough. It is not only in China that the traditional missionary venture has come or is coming to an end. Take the problem of recruitment: more have remarked on the fact that volunteers today are either scarce or curious, than that today no mission board can in fact offer any young person a life vocation on the mission field. In what country in the world is anyone prepared to predict with any confidence that Western missionaries will still be allowed to operate even ten years from now? Or to consider more agonizing matters: the United Church of Canada, for instance, was recently faced with an immense problem in Angola, where any trite answer that would seek to say glibly that Western imperialism is one thing and the preaching of the Christian faith is another, collapses. Why is Nkrumah, African nationalist that he is, who was brought up a Christian, reported to be considering leaving our faith? With what zest is an evangelist to make converts of Negroes who he now can predict may die as the price to be paid by *them* for *our* sins like 'apartheid'?

Since some persons in the Church at home seem not to realize the kind of feeling on these matters to be found in the non-Western world, I shall quote from the report of a Christian Missionary Activities Enquiry Committee appointed in 1954 by the state government of Madhya Pradesh in India. Among its Recommendations were the following:

> Those missionaries whose primary object is proselytization should be asked to withdraw. The large influx of foreign missionaries is undesirable and should be checked. . . .
> The use of medical or other professional service as a direct means of making conversions should be prohibited by law. . . .
> Any attempt by force or fraud, or threats of illicit means or grants of financial or other aid, or by fraudulent means or promises, or by moral and material assistance, or by taking advantage of any person's inexperience or confidence, or by exploiting any person's necessity, spiritual (mental) weakness or thoughtlessness, or, in general, any attempt or effort (whether successful or not), directly or indirectly to penetrate into the religious conscience of persons (whether of age or underage) of another faith, for the purpose of consciously altering their religious conscience

or faith, so as to agree with the ideas or convictions of the proselytizing party should be absolutely prohibited. . . .

An amendment of the Constitution of India may be sought, firstly, to clarify that the right of propagation has been given only to the citizens of India and secondly, that it does not include conversions brought about by force, fraud, or other illicit means.[1]

China, Angola, the Arab world after Suez, this sort of attitude in India, and the like are not simply illustrations of a practical problem. They are symptoms of an intellectual, emotional, and spiritual problem in which Christians are involved. That this is so is recognized even by the leading spokesman of what might be termed the conservative wing of modern missionary thinking, Hendrik Kraemer. In a recent article, he says: 'The present conditions and significance of the Muslim world as part of the present-day world as a whole have entered a new stage, the newness of which cannot easily be overestimated. The current Western evaluations and judgments about the Muslim world, in so far as they are derived from the past, are therefore necessarily outmoded'. He also speaks of 'the clumsiness and blindness with which Western public opinion, not excluding the opinion and attitude of responsible politicians and statesmen, reacts to the present situation and problems of the Muslim world. . . . The same is true in regard to the Christian Churches and their missionary concern in relation to the Muslim world'. He goes on:

The passing of the colonial era in the Muslim world, and the latter's ascendancy to independence and self-determi-

[1] As cited in Edmund Perry, *The Gospel in Dispute: the Relation of Christian Faith to Other Missionary Religions* (New York: 1958), pp. 18-19.

nation, are therefore of the greatest moment to all missionary leaders and servants of missions in the Muslim world. In saying this, I am not, in the first place, thinking of the difficult crises and threats of extinction through which the formerly established missions are going, and of which leaders and missionaries are fully aware. In using the words 'of great moment,' I am thinking in a line which seems not yet to have arisen before the eyes of most of the leaders and servants of formerly established missionary work in the Muslim world. Generally speaking, all attention and concern is turned toward defense of still tenable positions, toward discussion of ways to maintain in some form the effort and the witness. Frankly speaking, this seems to me to be a wrong orientation. Again, with full recognition of the sincere faithfulness behind these efforts of defense and maintenance, this wrong orientation betrays deafness to the voice of the sweeping turn in world-history and blindness to the *real* implications of missionary adequacy in the new situation. The time of Christian missions in the Muslim world, as the organized determined effort for converting Muslims and as inherited from the nineteenth century, is, as far as I see, *passed* in the postcolonial era.[2]

Few Western Christians have any inkling of the involvement of the Church within the object of anti-Westernism; or of the religious involvement of the resurgence in Asia and Africa of other communities. Of this resurgence we see usually only the political or economic facets, because these are the only ones that we can understand. The religious history of mankind is taking as monumental a turn in our century as is the political or

[2] 'Islamic Culture and Missionary Adequacy', *The Muslim World*, L (1960), 244, 245, 249-250.

economic, if only we could see it. And the upsurge of a vibrant and self-assertive 'new religious orientation of Buddhists and Hindus and the like evinces a new phase not merely in the history of those particular traditions, but in the history of the whole complex of man's religiousness, of which the Christian is a part, and an increasingly participant part. The traditional relation of the Christian Church to man's other religious traditions has been that of proselytizing evangelism, at least in theory. The end of that phase is the beginning of a new phase, in which the relation of the Church to other faiths will be new. But what it will be, in theory or practice, has yet to be worked out—not by the Church alone, but by the Church in its involvement with these others.

The missionary situation of the Church, then, is in profound crisis, in both practice and theory. The most vivid and most masterly summing up of this crisis is perhaps the brief remark of Canon Max Warren, the judicious and brilliant and sensitive and responsible General Secretary in London of the Church Missionary Society. His obituary on traditional mission policy and practice is in three sentences: 'We have marched around alien Jerichos the requisite number of times. We have sounded the trumpets. And the walls have not collapsed'.

Yet we promised that we would come back from the mission field to North America, and to theology. Traditio al missions are the exact extrapolation of the traditional theology of the Church. The passing of traditional missions is a supersession of one phase of the Church's traditional theology. The 'ecumenical' movements have been the result in part of pressures from the mission field because there the scandal of a divided Christendom came most starkly to light. It is from the mission field also that the scandal of a fundamental fallacy in traditional theology has been shown up. The rise of science in the nineteenth century induced a revision in Christian theology—what has sometimes been called the second Reformation. Some may think that Canon Warren exaggerates, but at least he calls attention to the seriousness of the new challenge, when he says that the impact of agnostic science will turn out to have been as child's play compared to the challenge to Christian theology of the faith of other men[3].

The woeful thing is that the meeting of that challenge has hardly seriously begun.

An illuminating story was told me recently by a Harvard friend, concerning Paul Tillich. Apparently a letter in the student paper, the *Harvard Crimson*, was able to show up as superficial in a particular case this eminent theologian's understanding of religious traditions in Asia. Some would perhaps find it not particularly surprising that an undergraduate these days should know more on this matter than a major Christian thinker. Until recently, certainly, it was not particularly expected that a man should know much, or indeed anything, about the religious life of other communities before he undertook to become a spokesman for his own. To me, however, the incident raises a significant issue. Looking at the matter historically, one may perhaps put it thus: probably Tillich belongs to the last generation of theologians who can formulate their conceptual system as religiously isolationist. The era of religious isolationism is about to be as much at an end as that of political isolationism al-

[3] In an address at Scarborough, Ontario, October 18, 1958.

ready is. The pith of Tillich's exposition has to do with its deliberate aptness to the intellectual context in which it appears: the correlation technique, of question and answer. But that context as he sees it is the mental climate of the Western world; and he has spoken to it just at the end of its separatist tradition, just before it is superseded by a new context, a climate modified radically by new breezes, or new storms, blowing in from the other parts of the planet. The new generation of the Church, unless it is content with a ghetto, will live in a cosmopolitan environment, which will make the work of even a Tillich appear parochial [4].

Ever since the impact of Greek philosophy on the Church, or shall we say the forced discovery of Greek philosophy by the Church, in the early centuries, every Christian theology has been written in the light of it. Whether the Christian thinker rejected or accepted it, modified or enriched it, he formulated his exposition aware of it, and aware that his readers would read him in the light of it. No serious intellectual statement of the Christian faith since that time has ignored this conceptual context.

Similarly, ever since the rise of science, the forced discovery of science by the Church, again subsequent Christian doctrine has been written in the light of it. Formulator and reader are aware of this context, and no intellectual statement that ignores it can be fully serious.

I suggest that we are about to enter a comparable situ-

[4] It is pleasant to report that since the above was set forth Dr. Tillich, having spent some time in Japan, has published in a booklet four lectures on *Christianity and the Encounter of the World Religions* (New York: Columbia University Press, 1963).

ation with regard to the other religious traditions of mankind. The time will soon be with us when a theologian who attempts to work out his position unaware that he does so as a member of a world society in which other theologians equally intelligent, equally devout, equally moral, are Hindus, Buddhists, Muslims, and unaware that his readers are likely perhaps to be Buddhists or to have Muslim husbands or Hindu colleagues—such a theologian is as out of date as is one who attempts to construct an intellectual position unaware that Aristotle has thought about the world or that existentialists have raised new orientations, or unaware that the earth is a minor planet in a galaxy that is vast only by terrestrial standards. Philosophy and science have impinged so far on theological thought more effectively than has comparative religion, but this will not last.

It is not my purpose in this essay to suggest the new theological systems that the Church will in the new situation bring forth. My task is to delineate the problems that such a system must answer, to try to analyse the context within which future theological thought will inescapably be set.

One of my theme songs in comparative-religion study is that man's religious diversity poses an intellectual problem, a moral problem, and a theological problem. In the rest of this essay I will consider the situation under these three heads—with emphasis on the last two. By 'intellectual' I mean at the academic level: the sheer challenge to the human mind to understand, when confronted as it is today with what appears at first to be the bewildering variety of man's religious life. At this level we have had or are having our Copernican Revolution, but not yet our

Newton. By this I mean that we have discovered the facts of our earth's being one of the planets, but have not yet explained them. The pew, if not yet the pulpit, the undergraduate if not yet the seminary professor, have begun to recognize not only that the Christian answers on man's cosmic quality are not the only answers, but even that the Christian questions are not the only questions. The awareness of multiformity is becoming vivid, and compelling.

Before Newton's day it used to be thought that we live in a radically dichotomous universe: there was our earth, where things fell to the ground, and there were the heavens, where things went round in circles. These were two quite different realms, and one did not think of confusing or even much relating the two. A profoundly significant step was taken when men recognized that the apple and the moon are in much the same kind of motion. Newton's mind was able to conceive an interpretation—accepted now by all of us, but revolutionary at the time—that without altering the fact that on earth things *do* fall to the ground and in the heavens things *do* go round in circles, yet saw both these facts as instances as a single kind of behaviour. In the religious field, the academic approach is similarly restless at the comparable dichotomy that for each group has in the past seen *our* tradition (whichever it be) as faith, other men's behaviour as superstition, the two realms to be explained in quite unrelated ways, understood on altogether separate principles. The Christian's faith has come down from God, the Buddhist's goes round in the circles of purely human aspiration; and so on. The intellectual challenge here is to make coherent sense, in a rational, integrated manner, of a wide range of apparently comparable and yet conspicuously diverse phenomena. And the academic world is closer to meeting this challenge than some theologians have noticed.

Certain Christians have even made the rather vigorous assertion that the Christian faith is *not* one of 'the religions of the world', that one misunderstands it if one attempts to see it in those terms. Most students of comparative religion have tended to pooh-pooh such a claim as unacceptable. I, perhaps surprisingly, take it very seriously indeed; but I have discovered recently that the same applies to the other traditions also. The Christian faith is not to be seen as a religion, one of the religions. But neither is the faith of Buddhists, Hindus, Muslims, or Andaman Islanders; and to think of it so is seriously to misunderstand and distort it. However, this is a large issue that I am currently writing a book about; forgive me for introducing it here, though I did think that the point might be illustrative[5]. I believe there is no question but that modern inquiry is showing that other men's faith is not so different from ours as we were brought up to suppose.

The intellectual problem, however, because of its essentially academic nature, we may leave aside now to pass on to the two issues from religious pluralism that are of moment to us professionally: to all Christians as Christians, and saliently to those of us who are charged to perceive conceptually and to formulate intellectually

[5] This book has since been completed and published, as *The Meaning and End of Religion* (New York: Macmillan, 1963).

the Christian faith as we ought to have it. These issues are what I have called the moral problem and the theological problem that religious diversity raises.

Religious diversity poses a moral problem because it disrupts community. It does so with new force in the modern world because divergent traditions that in the past did and could develop separately and insouciantly are to-day face to face; and, perhaps even more important and radical, are for the first time side by side. Different civilizations have in the past either ignored each other or fought each other; very occasionally in tiny ways perhaps they met each other. Today they not only meet but interpenetrate; they meet not only each other, but jointly meet joint problems, and must jointly try to solve them. They must collaborate. Perhaps the single most important challenge that mankind faces in our day is the need to turn our nascent world society into a world community.

This is not easy. In fact, the first effect of bringing diverse groups together, and particularly religiously diverse groups, is often conflict. This may be overt, or hidden. On the whole, as I have already remarked, I think that few Westerners, including Christians, have any inkling of how profound and bitter and massive, and also how much on the increase, is anti-Western feeling throughout the world; and in Africa and in Asia this is in many ways anti-Christian. Christian antagonism to outsiders is evident mostly in the realm of colour—though in more subtle ways it vitiates many other relations. There is also plenty of religious strife *among* the non-Christian traditions—as was explosively demonstrated in the Hindu-Muslim massacres around the partition of India.

Men have yet to learn our new task of living together as partners in a world of religious and cultural plurality. The technological and economic aspects of 'one world', of a humanity in process of global integration, are proceeding apace, and at the least are receiving the attention of many of our best minds and most influential groups. The political aspects also are under active and constant consideration, even though success here is not so evident, except in the supremely important day-to-day staving off of disaster. The ideological and cultural question of human cohesion, on the other hand, has received little attention, and relatively little progress can be reported; even though in the long run it may prove utterly crucial, and is already basic to much else. Unless men can learn to understand and to be loyal to each other across religious frontiers, unless we can build a world in which people profoundly of different faiths can live together and work together, then the prospects for our planet's future are not bright.

My own view is that the task of constructing even that minimum degree of world fellowship that will be necessary for man to survive at all is far too great to be accomplished on any other than a religious basis. From no other source than his faith, I believe, can man muster the energy, devotion, vision, resolution, the capacity to survive disappointment, that will be necessary—that *are* necessary—for this challenge. Cooperation among men of diverse religion is a moral imperative, even at the lowest level of social and political life.

127

Some would agree that the world community must have a religious basis, conceding that a lasting and peaceful society cannot be built by a group of men that are ultimately divided religiously, that have come to no mutual understanding; but would go on to hold that this is possible only if their own one tradition prevails. No doubt to some it would seem nice if all men were Roman Catholics, or Communists, or liberal universalists; or if all men would agree that religion does not really matter, or that it should be kept a private affair. Apart, however, from those that find such a vision inherently less appealing, many others will agree that for the moment it seems in any case hardly likely. Co-existence, if not a final truth of man's diversity, would seem at least an immediate necessity, and indeed, an immediate virtue.

If we must have rivalry among the religious communities of earth, might we not for the moment at least rival each other in our determination and capacity to promote reconciliation. Christians, Muslims, and Buddhists each believe that only *they* are able to do this. Rather than arguing this point ideologically, let us strive in a friendly race to see which can implement it most effectively and vigorously in practice—each recognizing that any success of the other is to be applauded, not decried.

There is, then, this general moral level of the imperative towards community, which in some sense all men of goodwill share—it is nonetheless insistent for that. We may move from that to the specifically Christian level. Here I have something very special to adduce. It is a thesis that I have been trying to develop for a couple of years now. The thesis essentially is this: that the emergence of the new world situation has brought to light a lack of integration in one area of Christian awareness, namely between the moral and the intellectual facets of our relations with our fellow men.

I begin with the affirmation that there are moral as well as conceptual implications of revealed truth. If we take seriously the revelation of God in Christ—if we really mean what we say when we affirm that his life, and his death on the cross, and his final triumph out of the very midst of self-sacrifice, embody the ultimate truth and power and glory of the universe—then two kinds of things follow, two orders of inference. On the moral level, there follows an imperative towards reconciliation, unity, harmony, and brotherhood. At this level, all men are included: we strive to break down barriers, to close up gulfs; we recognize all men as neighbours, as fellows, as sons of the universal father, seeking Him and finding Him, being sought by Him and being found by Him. At this level, we do not become truly Christian until we have reached out towards a community that turns all mankind into one total 'we'.

On the other hand, there is another level, the intellectual, the order of ideas, where it is the business of those of us who are theologians to draw out concepts, to construct doctrines. At this level, the doctrines that Christians have traditionally derived have tended to affirm a Christian exclusivism, a separation between those who believe and those who do not, a division of mankind into a 'we' and a 'they', a gulf between Christendom and the rest of the world: a gulf profound, ultimate, cosmic.

I shall come to the theological consideration of these theological ideas, in the third part of my paper. At the moment, I wish to consider the moral consequences of our theological ideas. Here my submission is that on this front the traditional doctrinal position of the Church has in fact militated against its traditional moral position, and has in fact encouraged Christians to approach other men immorally. Christ has taught us humility, but we have approached them with arrogance.

I do not say this lightly. This charge of arrogance is a serious one. It is my observation over more than twenty years of study of the Orient, and a little now of Africa, that the fundamental flaw of Western civilization in its role in world history is arrogance, and that this has infected also the Christian Church. If you think that I am being reckless or unwarranted here, ask any Jew, or read between the lines of the works of modern African or Asian thinkers.

May I take for illustration a phrase, not unrepresentative, which was under discussion recently by the United Church of Canada's commission on faith, and which ran as follows: 'Without the particular knowledge of God in Jesus Christ, men do not really know God at all'. Let us leave aside for the moment any question of whether or not this is true. We shall return to that presently. My point here is simply that, in any case, it is arrogant. At least, it becomes arrogant when one carries it out to the non-Western world. In the quiet of the study, it may be possible for the speculative mind to produce this kind of doctrine, provided that one keep it purely bookish. But except at the cost of insensitivity or delinquence, it is morally not possible actually to go out into the world and say to devout, intelligent, fellow human beings: 'We are saved and you are damned'; or, 'We believe that we know God, and we are right; you believe that you know God, and you are totally wrong'.

This is intolerable from merely human standards. It is doubly so from Christian ones. Any position that antagonizes and alienates rather than reconciles, that is arrogant rather than humble, that promotes segregation rather than brotherhood, that is unlovely, is *ipso facto* un-Christian.

There is a further point at which the traditional position seems to me morally un-Christian. From the notion that if Christianity is true, then other religions must be false (a notion whose *logic* I shall challenge later), it is possible to go on to the converse proposition: that if anyone else's faith turns out to be valid or adequate, then it would follow that Christianity must be false—a form of logic that has, in fact, driven many from their own faith, and indeed from any faith at all. If one's chances of getting to Heaven—or to use a nowadays more acceptable metaphor, of coming into God's presence—are dependent upon other people's not getting there, then one becomes walled up within the quite intolerable position that the Christian has a vested interest in other men's damnation. It is shocking to admit it, but this actually takes place. When an observer comes back from Asia, or from a study of Asian religious traditions, and reports that, contrary to accepted theory, some Hindus and Buddhists and some Muslims lead a pious and moral life and seem very near to God by any possible standard, so that, so far as one can see, in these particular cases at least faith is as 'adequate' as Christian faith, then presumably a Christian should be overjoyed, enthusiastically hopeful that this be true, even though he might be permitted a fear lest it not be so. Instead, I have sometimes witnessed just the opposite: an emotional resistance to the news, men hoping firmly that it is not so, though perhaps with a covert fear that it might be. Whatever the rights and wrongs of the situation theoretically, I submit that practically this is just not Christian, and indeed is not tolerable. It will not do, to have a faith that can be undermined by God's saving one's neighbour; or to be afraid lest other men turn out to be closer to God than one had been led to suppose.

Let us turn, finally, to the theological problem, that the existence of other religious communities poses for the Christian (and that to-day's new immediate and face-to-face awareness of their existence poses urgently). This problem began, in a compelling form, with the discovery of America, and the concomitant discovery of men on this continent who therefore had been 'out of reach of the gospel'. In theory the peoples of Africa and Asia could have heard the gospel story and could have believed it and been saved. If they had not become Christian, this could be interpreted as due to their cussedness, or to Christian lethargy in not evangelizing them, and so on. But with the discovery of redskins in America who had lived for fifteen centuries since Christ died, unable to be saved through faith in him, many sensitive theologians were bewildered.

In our day a comparable problem is presented, and may be viewed in two ways. First, how does one account, theologically, for the fact of man's religious diversity? This is really as big an issue, almost, as the question of how one accounts theologically for evil—

but Christian theologians have been much more conscious of the fact of evil than that of religious pluralism. Another way of viewing it is to phrase a question as to whether or how far or how non-Christians are saved, or know God. The former question has got, so far as I know, almost no serious answers of any kind. The latter has found a considerable number of attempted answers, though to my taste none of these is at all satisfactory.

On the former point I would simply like to suggest that from now on any serious intellectual statement of the Christian faith must include, if it is to serve its purpose among men, some sort of doctrine of other religions. We explain the fact that the Milky Way is there by the doctrine of creation, but how do we explain the fact that the Bhagavad Gita is there?

This would presumably include also an answer to our second question. Here I would like merely to comment on one of the answers that have in fact been given. It is the one that we have already mentioned: 'Without the particular knowledge of God in Jesus Christ, men do not really know God at all'. First, of course, one must recognize the positive point that this intellectualization stems from and attempts to affirm the basic and ultimate and of course positive faith of the Church that in Christ God died for us men and our salvation, that through faith in him we are saved. In the new formulations to which we may look forward, this positive faith must be preserved. Yet in the negative proposition as framed, one may see a number of difficulties, and one may suppose that the force of these will come to be increasingly felt in coming decades.

First, there is an epistemological difficulty. How could one possibly know?

If one asks how we know the Christian faith to be true, there are perhaps two kinds of answer. First, we ourselves find in our lives, by accepting and interiorizing it and attempting to live in accordance with it, that it proves itself. We know it to be true because we have lived it. Secondly, one may answer that for now almost two thousand years the Church has proven it and found it so—hundreds of millions of people, of all kinds and in all circumstances and in many ages, have staked their lives upon it, and have found it right. On the other hand, if one is asked how one knows the faith of people in other traditions to be false, one is rather stumped.

Most people who make this kind of statement do not in fact know much about the matter. Actually the only basis on which their position can and does rest is a logical inference. It seems to them a theoretical implication of what they themselves consider to be true, that other peoples' faith *must* be illusory. Personally, I think that this is to put far too much weight on logical implication. There have been innumerable illustrations of man's capacity for starting from some cogent theoretical position and then inferring from it logically something else that at the time seems to him persuasive but that in fact turns out on practical investigation not to hold. It is far too sweeping to condemn the great majority of mankind to lives of utter meaninglessness and perhaps to Hell, simply on the basis of what seems to some individuals the force of logic. Part of what the Western world has been doing for the last four centuries has been learning to get away from this kind of reliance on purely logical structures, totally untested by experience or by any other consideration. The damnation of my neighbour is too weighty a matter to rest on a syllogism.

Secondly, there is the problem of empirical observation. One cannot be anything but tentative here, of course, and inferential. Yet so far as actual observation goes, the evidence would seem overwhelming that in fact individual Buddhists, Hindus, Muslims, and others have known, and do know, God. I personally have friends from these communities whom it seems to me preposterous to think about in any other way. (If we do not have friends among these communities, we should probably refrain from generalizations about them.)

This point, however, presumably need not be laboured. The position set forth has obviously not been based, and does not claim to be based, upon empirical observation. If one insists on holding it, it must be held *against* the evidence of empirical observation. This can be done, as a recent writer has formulated it:

> The Gospel of Jesus Christ comes to us with a built-in prejudgment of all other faiths so that we know in advance of our study what we must ultimately conclude about them. They give meanings to life apart from that which God has given in the biblical story culminating with Jesus Christ, and they organize life outside the covenant community of Jesus Christ. Therefore, devoid of this saving knowledge and power of God, these faiths not only are unable to bring men to God, they actually lead men away from God and hold them captive from God. This definitive and blanket judgment . . . is not derived from our

investigation of the religions but is given in the structure and content of Gospel faith itself.[6]

Again, a careful study by a neo-orthodox trainer of missionaries in Basel, Dr. Kellerhals, says that Islam, like other 'foreign religions', is a 'human attempt to win God for oneself, . . . to catch Him and confine Him on the plane of one's own spiritual life, . . . and for oneself to hold Him fast' [7]. He knows this, he says explicitly, nòt from a study of Islam but before he begins that study, from his Christian premises; he knows it by revelation, and therefore he can disdain all human argument against it. The position seems thoroughly logical, and once one has walled oneself up within it, impregnable. Those of us who, *after* our study of Islam or of Indian or Chinese religion, and after our fellowship with Muslims and other personal friends, have come to know that these religious traditions are not that, but are channels through which God Himself comes into touch with these His children—what answer can we give?

One possible answer is that empirical knowledge does in the end have to be reckoned with, does in the end win out even over conviction that claims for itself the self-certification of revelation. We do not deny that upholders of this sort of position are recipients of revelation, genuinely; but we would argue that the revelation itself is not propositional, and that their interpretation of the revelation that they have received is their own, is human

[6] Perry, *op. cit.,* p. 83.

[7] Emanuel Kellerhals, *Der Islam: seine Geschichte, seine Lehre, sein Wesen,* 2d ed. (Basel and Stuttgart, 1956), pp. 15-16. Translation mine.

and fallible, is partial, and in this case is in some ways wrong.

In fact, we have been through all this before. A hundred years ago the Christian argued that he knew by divine revelation that the earth was but six thousand years old and that evolution did not happen, and therefore any evidence that geologists or biologists might adduce to the contrary need not be taken seriously. A repentant Church still claims revelation but now admits that its former theology needed revision. In the twentieth century the increasing evidence that the faith of men in other religious communities is not so different from our own as we have traditionally asserted it to be, although it is forcing some to abandon any faith in revelation at all, will in general, we predict, force us rather to revise our theological formulations.

Finally, even on the side of internal Christian doctrine the exclusivist position is theoretically difficult. For according to traditional Christian doctrine, there is not only one person in the Trinity, namely Christ, but three persons: God the Father, God the Son, and God the Holy Spirit. Is God not Creator? If so, then is He not to be known—however impartially, distortedly, inadequately—in creation? Is He not active in history? If so, is His spirit totally absent from any history, including even the history of other men's faith?

It may be argued that outside the Christian tradition men may know God in part, but cannot know Him fully. This is undoubtedly valid, but the apparent implications are perhaps precarious. For one may well ask: Is it possible for a Christian to know God fully? I personally do not see what it might mean to say that any man, Christian or other, has a complete knowledge of God. This would certainly be untenable this side of the grave, at the very least? The finite cannot comprehend the infinite.

What does one actually mean when one speaks of the knowledge of God? It has been said, and I think rightly, that the only true atheist is he who loves no one and whom no one loves; who is blind to all beauty and all justice; who knows no truth; and who has lost all hope.

Christians know God only in part. But one part of their knowing Him is the recognition that He does not leave any of us utterly outside His knowledge.

It is easier, however, of course, to demolish a theological position than to construct an alternative one. The fallacy of relentless exclusivism is becoming more obvious than is the right way of reconciling a truly Christian charity and perceptivity with doctrinal adequacy. On this matter I personally have a number of views, but the one about which I feel most strongly is that this matter is important—while the rest of my particular views on it are not necessarily so. In other words, I am much more concerned to stress the fact that the Church must work, and work vigorously, and work on a large scale, in order to construct an adequate doctrine in this realm (which in my view it has never yet elaborated), than I am concerned to push my own particular suggestions. Most of all I would emphasize that whether or not my particular construction seems inadequate, the position formulated above from which I strongly dissent must in any case be seen to be inadequate also.

Having expressed this caution, I may nonetheless make

one or two suggestions. First, I rather feel that the final doctrine on this matter may perhaps run along the lines of affirming that a Buddhist who is saved, or a Hindu or a Muslim or whoever, is saved, and is saved only, because God is the kind of God whom Jesus Christ has revealed Him to be. This is not exclusivist; indeed, it coheres, I feel, with the points that I have made above in dissenting from exclusivism. If the Christian revelation were *not* true, then it might be possible to imagine that God would allow Hindus to worship Him or Muslims to obey Him or Buddhists to feel compassionate towards their fellows, without His responding, without His reaching out to hold them in His arms. But because God is what He is, because He is what Christ has shown Him to be, *therefore* other men *do* live in His presence. Also, therefore we (as Christians) know this to be so.

I rather wonder whether the fundamental difficulty in the formulated position, and in all similar statements, does not arise somehow from an anthropocentric emphasis that it surreptitiously implies. To talk of man's knowing God is to move in the realm of thinking of religion as a human quest, and of knowledge of God as something that man attains, or even achieves. Of course it does not state it thus, but it skirts close to implying somehow that we are saved by *our* doings (or knowings). Must one not rather take the Christian doctrine of grace more seriously? The question must be more adequately phrased: Does God let Himself be known only to those to whom He has let Himself be known through Christ? Does God love only those who respond to Him in this tradition?

We are not saved by our knowledge; we are not saved

by our membership in the Church; we are not saved by anything of *our* doing. We are saved rather by the only thing that could possibly save us, the anguish and the love of God. While we have no final way of knowing with assurance how God deals or acts in other men's lives, and therefore cannot make any final pronouncement (such as the formulator of the position stated has attempted to make), nonetheless we must perhaps at least be hesitant in setting boundaries to that anguish and that love.

The God whom we have come to know, so far as we can sense His action, reaches out after all men everywhere, and speaks to all who will listen. Both within and without the Church men listen all too dimly. Yet both within and without the Church, so far as we can see, God does somehow enter into men's hearts.

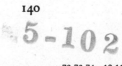

72 73 74   12 11 10 9 8 7 6 5 4 3 2